Basic CROCHETING

All the Skills and Tools You Need to Get Started

Sharon Hernes Silverman

Annie Modesitt,
consultant

photographs by
Alan Wycheck

illustrations by
Marjorie Leggitt

STACKPOLE
BOOKS

0 11557 03316 8

Copyright © 2006 by Stackpole Books

Published by
STACKPOLE BOOKS
5067 Ritter Road
Mechanicsburg, PA 17055
www.stackpolebooks.com

Printed in China

10 9 8 7 6 5 4 3 2 1

FIRST EDITION

Photographs by Alan Wycheck
Illustrations by Marjorie Leggitt
Cover design by Tracy Patterson

Hat, mittens, and scarf patterns © Annie Modesitt. Used with permission of the designer. All other patterns © Sharon Hernes Silverman

Crochet Abbreviations Master List, Skill Levels for Crocheting, Standard Body Measurements/Sizing, and Standard Yarn Weight System charts used courtesy of the Craft Yarn Council of America (CYCA), www.yarnstandards.com.

Library of Congress Cataloging-in-Publication Data

Basic crocheting : all the skills and tools you need to get started / Sharon Hernes Silverman.
     p. cm.
Includes index.
ISBN-13: 978-0-8117-3316-8 (spiral bound pb)
ISBN-10: 0-8117-3316-5 (spiral bound pb)
1. Crocheting—Patterns. I. Silverman, Sharon Hernes.
TT820.B365 2006
746.43'4—dc22

2005037862

Contents

Acknowledgments iv
Introduction v

Part I: Basic Tools and Skills

1. Tools and Materials 2
   Yarn 2
   Hooks 4
   Other Equipment 5

2. Basic Skills 7
   Preparing Yarn for Use 7
   Holding the Hook 9
   Healthy Crocheting 9
   Making a Slip Knot 10
   Holding the Yarn 12
   Chain Stitch 12
   Removing Extra Chains 14
   Slip Stitch 15
   Single Crochet 16
   Half Double Crochet 18
   Double Crochet 20
   Working in Rows 23
   Joining a New Yarn 24
   Fastening Off 26
   Weaving in Ends 26
   Measuring Gauge 27
   Blocking 27
   Reading a Pattern 28

Part II: Projects

1. Shadowbox Pillow 30
   Skill Workshop: Adding a New Color
        and Turning a Corner 34
   Skill Workshop: Lacing a Pillow 36

2. Jewel Tone Poncho 38
   Skill Workshop: Windowpane 42
   Skill Workshop: Fringe 43

3. Basketweave Blanket 45
   Skill Workshop: Basketweave (Front Raised
        and Back Raised Double Crochet Stitches) . . 49
   Skill Workshop: Blanket Trim 51

4. Horizontal Scarf 53
   Skill Workshop: Integral Fringe 57

5. Bunny Basket 58
   Skill Workshop: Crocheting in the Round . . 62
   Skill Workshop: Handle and Finishing 64

6. Child's Watch Cap 65
   Skill Workshop: Working in Back
        Loop Only 70
   Skill Workshop: Joining Hatband 71

7. Child's Mittens 72
   Skill Workshop: Making a Thumb Gusset
        and Thumb 76

8. Openwork Placemats 78
   Skill Workshop: Filet Crochet 83
   Skill Workshop: Trim 85

9. Woven Shoulder Bag 86
   Skill Workshop: Woven Stitch 91
   Skill Workshop: Decreasing Single Crochet . . 92
   Skill Workshop: Handbag Assembly 93

10. Wavy Sweater 95
    Skill Workshop: Wavy Chevron Stitch 100
    Skill Workshop: Sweater Assembly and
         Neckline Trim 102

Appendices 105
   Crocheting Abbreviations Master List 105
   Skill Levels for Crocheting 105
   Standard Body Measurements/Sizing 106
   Standard Yarn Weight System 110

Resources 111
   Books
   Yarn and Crocheting Supplies
   Other Resources for Crocheters

Acknowledgments

Being invited to write *Basic Crocheting* for Stackpole Books was a dream come true. Many people offered help and encouragement:

Annie Modesitt, known for her knitting and crocheted designs and her own published work, submitted patterns for the hat, mittens, and scarf. Annie was a delightful collaborator. Her website, www.anniemodesitt.com, is an inspiration.

Photographer Alan Wycheck spent several days in the studio and at his computer making sure the pictures were just right. Beginning crocheters will benefit greatly from Alan's persistence in making sure every action is clearly visible.

Terri McClure demonstrated many crocheting techniques for the camera. Her neat work, helpful suggestions, and stamina in the studio are a big part of the project's success.

Illustrator Marjorie Leggitt produced the detailed drawings that appear in this volume. Marjorie has rendered illustrations that are technical and beautiful, and which are sure to be valuable to new crafters.

Thanks to Mary Colucci, Executive Director of the Craft Yarn Council of America, for permission to reprint charts of yarn industry standards.

The Crochet Guild of America (CGOA) provides a wealth of information, including *Crochet!* magazine, newsletters, and online instruction. Their conferences offer crocheters a chance to take classes, share tips, and shop for yarn and related products. CGOA has been a wonderful resource for me.

Leigh Ann Berry Chow, editor of *Basic Knitting*, provided helpful project management advice.

Mark Allison, Editor, and Judith M. Schnell, Publisher and Vice President of Stackpole Books, were supportive and enthusiastic from our first meeting through the book's completion. The design wizardry of Tracy Patterson and Caroline Stover made this volume both visually appealing and easy to follow. Thanks also to Amy D. Lerner and Amy Wagner for their editorial expertise. This project gave me many hours of pleasure, both in the crafting and in the interaction with the staff at Stackpole.

Thanks to my husband, Alan Silverman, and our sons, Jason and Steven, for their love and encouragement and for putting up with all of the yarn. Other family members and friends also lent their support, which means more to me than I can ever express. Special thanks to Janet Napoli, my forever friend, for her support and the chocolate.

I am grateful to my mother, Babe Hernes, for teaching me how to crochet when I was about ten years old. Thanks, Mom, for putting some yarn and a hook in my hand.

Introduction

Crocheting is an ancient technique that has evolved into the perfect contemporary craft. It's fun, easy to learn, and versatile. Basic stitches, used in innovative combinations with the fabulous variety of yarn available today, create stylish designs far removed from the doilies and granny squares of yesteryear.

Basic Crocheting is a comprehensive introduction to the skills you need to become a crocheter. The first half of the book teaches the fundamental techniques and stitches. The second half shows you how to use those skills to create actual projects. Skill workshops that accompany each project focus on specific techniques relevant to that item. Designs were selected to give you a wide range of choices for what to make, from apparel to articles for the home.

Even experienced crocheters are sometimes frustrated by patterns that are hard to understand or seem to leave out a key instruction. To make sure you do not experience this disappointment, *Basic Crocheting* provides detailed instructions for every step, supplemented with helpful photographs and illustrations.

Start out by working through the Basic Skills section, practicing the techniques until you are comfortable with them. Soon you will be ready to move onto the projects and create your own beautifully handcrafted items.

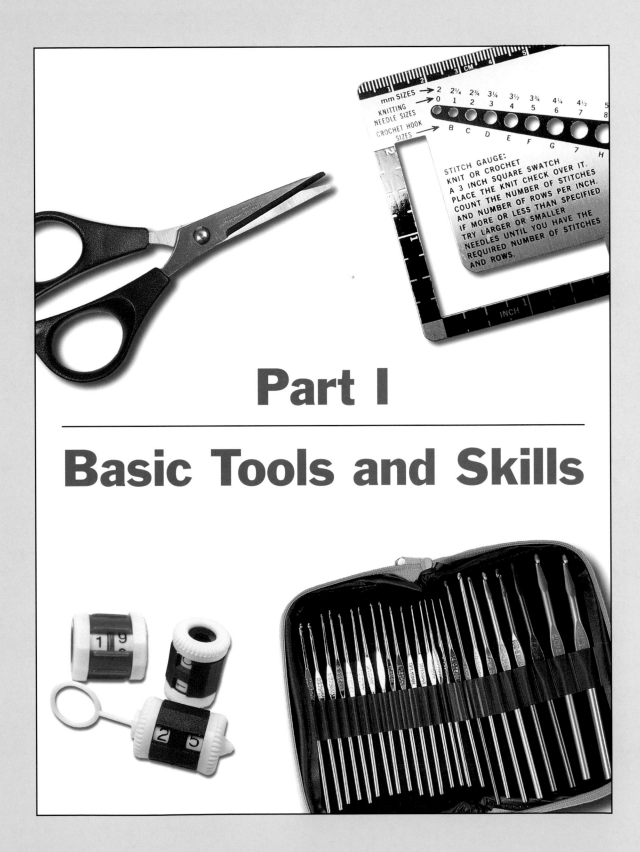

Part I

Basic Tools and Skills

Yarn

COLOR

Yarn comes in a dazzling array of colors. Variegated yarns combine several hues in one skein, changing from one color to another along the yarn. A visit to your local yarn store or craft shop is sure to inspire you with its rainbow of colors.

Most yarn is dyed commercially in batches, or lots. The color can vary from one batch to another. To avoid color discrepancies, purchase enough yarn to complete your project. Check the codes on the skeins' labels to make sure the yarn is all the same color and is from the same dye lot.

It is easier to see the stitches with light-colored yarn than with darker colors.

The CYCA's six yarn weight categories (see also the standard yarn weight system appendix): Super Fine, Fine, Light, Medium, Bulky, Super Bulky

WEIGHT

Yarn also comes in different weights, from super fine to super bulky. A crochet pattern will specify the type of yarn you should use. To make the finished project look like the designer intended, use the recommended weight.

The Craft Yarn Council of America (CYCA) has issued yarn weight standards. These guidelines organize yarn into six weight categories. Finer yarns are well-suited to baby items and other delicate pieces; bulkier yarns lend themselves to thick, heavy sweaters. If you ever want to substitute one yarn for another, make sure that it is in the same weight category.

COMPOSITION AND STRUCTURE

Yarn is made of spun fibers. These can be natural, such as wool, mohair, silk, or cotton; synthetic, such as acrylic, nylon, or polyester; or a blend. Each fiber has its own characteristics. Wool, for example, is warm but not as strong as some other fibers; acrylic is durable but not as breathable as natural materials. Blended yarns can provide the best of both worlds. Creative new blends—incorporating materials such as Tencel, camel's hair, even soybean fibers—are being developed all the time.

The word *ply* means how many strands are twisted together to make the yarn or thread. *Mercerized* cotton is thread that has processed to preshrink it, add luster, and help it hold dye.

The way a yarn's fibers are spun determines its structure. Here are some examples:

Spiral: Thinner yarn twisted around a thicker yarn.

Chenille: Plush, velvety pile. Comes from the French word for caterpillar.

Bouclé: Curled or twisted yarn held together in a way that produces small loops on the surface, giving it a kinky appearance and a springy feel.

Nubby: Two strands twisted so that one overlaps the other to produce a bumpy texture.

Slubby: A strand that is alternately thick and thin, twisted with a smooth or a slubby second strand.

Tape: Yarn made of knitted threads woven into a narrow, flat band.

Novelty yarns: These can have "eyelash" threads, metallic threads, faux fur or feathers, ladder or railroad tracks effects, sequins . . . you name it. Some can be used solo; others work best when combined with another yarn.

Almost any stringlike material can be crocheted. Try your hand with gift-wrapping ribbon, raffia, fishing line, strips of rags, or plastic gimp to see what you like.

Hooks

The crochet hook is your basic tool. All have a hook on one end, which is used to pull loops through the work. Many have a flat part in the middle for you to grip. Cushioned hooks are also available. Hooks are made in steel, aluminum, plastic, wood, bamboo, and bone. They are sized by the diameter of the shaft.

Hooks are sold individually or in sets.

Crochet Hook Sizes

Millimeter Range	U.S. Size Range*
2.25 mm	B-1
2.75 mm	C-2
3.25 mm	D-3
3.5 mm	E-4
3.75 mm	F-5
4 mm	G-6
4.5 mm	7
5 mm	H-8
5.5 mm	I-9
6 mm	J-10
6.5 mm	K-10½
8 mm	L-11
9 mm	M/N-13
10 mm	N/P-15
15 mm	P/Q
16 mm	Q
19 mm	S

*Letter or number may vary. Millimeter sizing is the most accurate.

Other Equipment

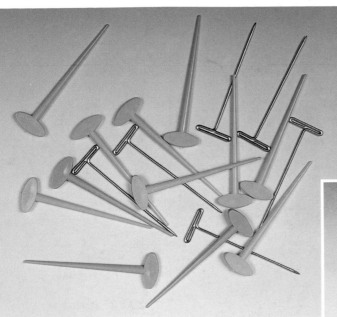

PINS
Used to hold finished pieces in place for blocking and for holding pieces in position when sewing seams.

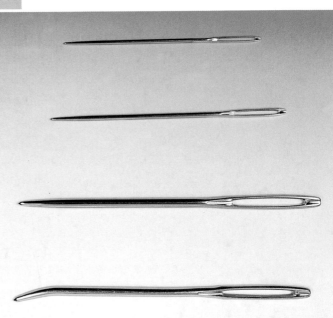

TAPESTRY NEEDLES
Used to sew seams and close rounds (like at the top of a hat).

SCISSORS AND YARN CUTTER
Used to cut yarn. The pendant has a recessed blade accessible through the notched edges. This is useful to take on an airplane when scissors are not allowed.

TAPE MEASURE
Used to measure people to determine garment size, and to measure work to check how a garment fits. Can also use to check gauge.

5

HOOK/STITCH GAUGE

Used to measure the gauge of a crocheted swatch, and to identify the size of unlabeled hooks.

ROW COUNTERS

Used to keep track of rows. This is especially useful if you get interrupted while you're working. Alternatively, use a pencil and paper to log your progress as you go along.

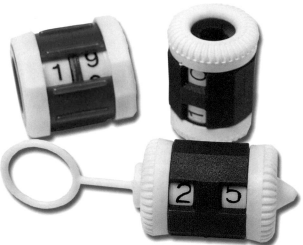

STEAM IRON OR STEAMER

Used to block finished items before assembly or on finished pieces.

COILLESS SAFETY PINS

Used to mark the beginning of a round or the position of a stitch without getting caught in the yarn.

Preparing Yarn for Use

Most commercially manufactured yarn comes in machine-wound oblong skeins. You do not need to take off the label, also called the ball band, to use the yarn. It will pull from the middle of the skein. If the label indicates which side to pull from, follow those instructions. If not, you will have to find the correct end, tucked into the skein. Reach inside with a couple of fingers (kind of like you are pulling the giblets from a Thanksgiving turkey) to feel for the end. Pull gently. If the yarn pulls cleanly from the center, you have found the right end. If the yarn starts to tighten the skein around the outside, you are using the wrong end. Don't worry if you get a small clump along with the working yarn. Simply stuff the excess back in after you find the end.

Always save the labels. They contain washing and care instructions and will be useful if you want to make another project. A good way to store them is in a photo album. Slip them under the clear pages along with any notes you have about the yarn or the project.

Cotton crochet thread comes on cardboard cylinders or cones. The thread unwinds from the outside in. Locate the end of the cotton, which is usually tucked under a few of the outer strands, and use it from there.

Hanks of yarn are large circular loops folded into a figure-eight and tied to hold them in place. Hand-dyed yarns and natural fiber yarns made in small batches are often wound this way because being made into skeins could crease the yarn permanently. You should not crochet directly from a hank; make it into a ball first.

It is worth it to take the time to make a ball. A tangled mass of yarn can take hours to unsnarl, or it can become so knotted that it must be discarded.

1. Remove the small ties and untwist the hank into one big loop. Put the loop over the back of a chair, or have a friend hold the loop around both of his or her outstretched hands.

Keep the yarn nice and relaxed as you wind it. Do not pull or stretch it. The ball should be slightly squishy, not rock hard.

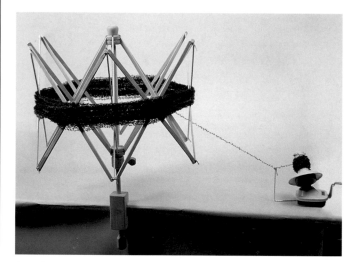

An alternative is to use a ball winder/yarn swift, designed to wind hanks into balls. Yarn shops usually have these for sale and may even offer to wind your yarn into balls at the shop for free on their own equipment.

2. Take the end of the yarn and start winding it into a ball. Wind it around your fingers for the first few rounds, and then wind the yarn around the growing ball. Turn the ball as it grows so the yarn forms a nice round shape as you wind it.

Holding the Hook

You can hold a crochet hook like a pencil or a knife.

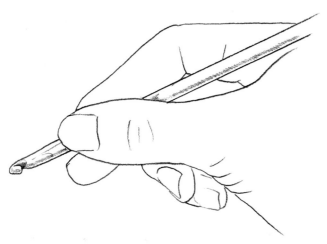

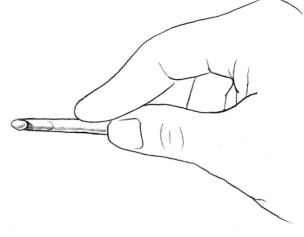

To hold like a pencil, put your thumb and index finger over the flat section of the hook. The end of the shaft rests on the top of your hand.

To hold like a knife, grab the hook from the top. Slide your index finger toward the hook. The end of the shaft is under your palm.

Healthy Crocheting

Crocheting is not strenuous, but it is physical and uses repetitive motions. To avoid strain and injury, it is important to work comfortably and not to do too much, especially at first. Here are some guidelines for healthy crocheting:

- Use a chair with good back support.
- Don't try to hold a heavy project, like a blanket, as it gets unwieldy. Work at a surface where you can lay the project down.
- Use adequate lighting.
- Use reading glasses or a magnifier on a stand if necessary.
- Take a break every 20 to 30 minutes to walk around, stretch your neck, arms, and legs, and give your eyes a rest.
- If you ever feel pain or discomfort while crocheting, STOP.

If you are left-handed, this is what the pencil hold should look like.

If you are left-handed, this is what the knife hold should look like. (Left-handers can look at any instructional drawings or photos in a mirror to see the proper position for them. Another alternative is to scan an image and flip it left to right.) When working with and learning from a right-handed crocheter, sit facing each other. Your work will be a mirror image of hers.

Making a Slip Knot

A slip knot attaches the yarn to the hook so you can begin to crochet. It is different than a "slip stitch."

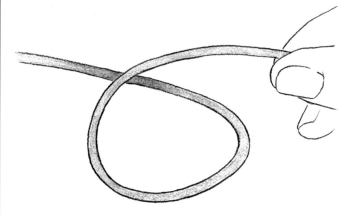

Make a loop of yarn. The working end is on top.

Now take the working end and tuck it under the loop to make a pretzel shape.

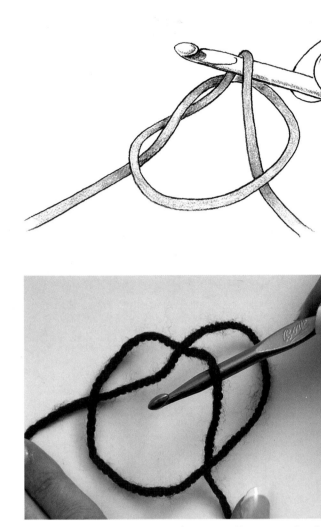

Using your hook, go over the pretzel's top circle, then put the hook under the center yarn to grab it.

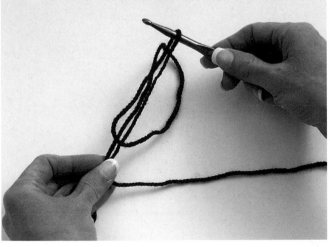

Begin to pull up, holding onto both ends of the yarn with your other hand. This starts to tighten the slip knot.

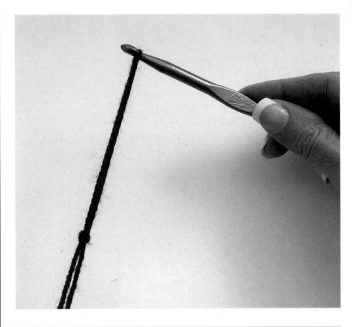

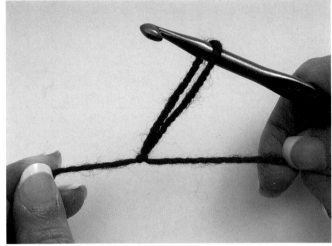

Once the knot tightens, pull the two ends apart to move the knot close to the hook.

The slip knot is complete.

11

Holding the Yarn

Successful crocheting depends on having the right tension on the yarn. This is achieved with the hand that is not holding the hook. The yarn has to flow over that hand and be controlled by it at the same time.

Here is one way to hold the yarn. The third, fourth, and fifth fingers hold the yarn in place lightly. Do not grip the yarn tightly with those fingers, or you will feel like you are tugging the yarn and your stitches will be too tight to use.

This is only one suggestion for how to hold yarn. If another position is more comfortable for you, use it. The important thing is to maintain even tension as you work.

The photo shows the left hand palm up to indicate the position of the yarn. Hold your palm down with the fingers closed when you crochet.

Chain Stitch

Chain stitches (abbreviated ch) serve as the first row, or foundation row, for the rest of the work.

1. Wrap the yarn over (abbreviated yo) the hook from back to front, between the loop that's already on there and the hook. Hold the tail of the yarn in your palm (but not too tight). If you do not hold it, the loop will spin around and you will not be able to make the stitch. At the same time, don't pull the loop that's on the hook too tight. This is the tricky part! Be patient and you will get the hang of it.

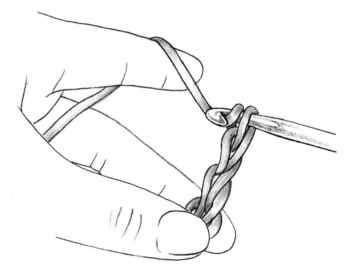

Here are some completed chain stitches. Practice your technique until you can make chains evenly. Your stitches should all be the same size and have the same tension. Keep your hands relaxed as you work.

2. Use the hook to pull the yarn you just wrapped around the hook through the loop. This completes one chain stitch. Remember, do not pull with your hook hand too tightly, or you will make the loop too small.

3. As you add to the chain, pinch the finished part lightly between your thumb and third finger of the non-hook hand. Move your thumb and third finger closer to the hook after completing 3 to 4 stitches. This helps keep the proper tension on your work and prevents the chain from curling.

Removing Extra Chains

It's frustrating to make a long chain foundation, only to discover at the end of the next row that you didn't make enough chain stitches. For this reason, some of the patterns recommend that you make a few extra chains just in case. They are easy to take out later.

Here is an example of an item that has too many chains in the foundation row.

1. Begin to unknot the extra chains by hand.

2. Continue to undo the extra chains until you get rid of all the unwanted stitches.

3. When you have taken out the extra stitches, give the tail a light tug. The rest of the stitches will not unravel.

Slip Stitch

The low-profile slip stitch (abbreviated sl st) is often used to join a new yarn to a piece, or to form a length of chain stitches into a ring.

1. Find the stitch where you will insert the hook. Each pattern will tell you how many stitches away from the hook you should insert it. In this photo, it is the second one from the hook, right above the thumbnail. Because you are working into chain stitches, notice that you push the hook through only the top loop of the chain. (On subsequent rows when you are working into other types of stitches, you will work through both loops of those stitches.)

2. Push the hook through that stitch from front to back. Hold onto the finished work, or length of chains, with your other hand to keep it from spinning and making it impossible to make the stitch.

3. Wrap the yarn over (yo) the hook from back to front.

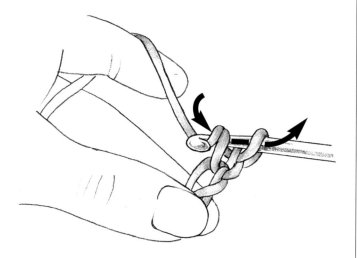

4. Pull the yarn through both of the loops on the hook.

5. This completes the slip stitch.

To summarize: Insert hook, wrap yarn around hook, pull through both loops.

Single Crochet

The single crochet stitch (abbreviated sc) is used in many of the projects in this book. Since it is not as "leggy" as double crochet and other tall stitches, single crochet is ideal when you want a tighter, more dense look. When working with other stitches in combination, it gives a nice texture.

1. Find the stitch where you will insert the hook. In this photo, it is the second one from the hook, as indicated by the needle. If you are working into chain stitches, push the hook through only the top loop of the chain. If you are working into stitches other than chains, push the hook below both loops in the stitches.

2. Push the hook through that stitch from front to back. Hold onto the finished work with your other hand to keep it from spinning and making it impossible to make the stitch.

3. Wrap the yarn over (yo) the hook from back to front.

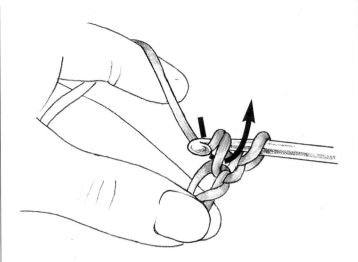

4. So far it is just like a slip stitch. But now, instead of pulling through both loops like in a sl st, you will pull the yarn through just one of the loops on the hook. This leaves two loops remaining on the hook.

5. Wrap the yarn over the hook from back to front.

6. Pull through both of the loops on the hook.

17

7. This completes the single crochet stitch.

8. Here is a row of completed single crochet stitches.

To summarize: Insert hook, wrap yarn around hook, pull through to front, wrap yarn around hook, pull through two remaining loops.

Half Double Crochet

The half double crochet stitch (hdc) is taller than a single crochet but not as tall as a double. It works up fast and easy and is a versatile and attractive stitch. Unlike in the single crochet, the yarn is wrapped around the hook before the hook is inserted into a stitch.

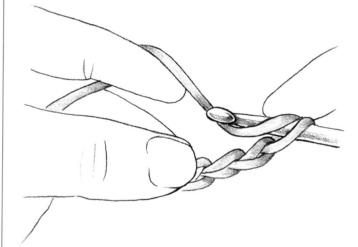

1. Wrap the yarn over the hook from back to front. Find the stitch where you will insert the hook. In the photo, it is the empty stitch next to the two (turning) chains. If you are working into already-made stitches like in this example, push the hook through both loops of the stitch. If you are working into the foundation chain, use only the top loop.

2. Push the hook through that stitch from front to back. Hold onto the finished work with your other hand to keep it from spinning and making it impossible to make the stitch. Use your hook hand to keep the loops on the hook from turning.

3. Wrap the yarn over (yo) the hook again from back to front.

4. Pull the yarn through to the front. This leaves three loops remaining on the hook.

5. Wrap the yarn over the hook again from back to front.

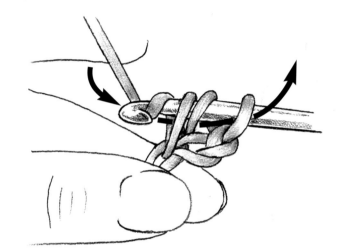

19

6. Pull through all three loops.

7. This completes the half double crochet.

8. The top row in this swatch is row of completed half double crochet stitches.

To summarize: Wrap the yarn around the hook. Insert hook into stitch. Wrap yarn around the hook. Pull to front. Wrap again. Pull through all three loops.

Double Crochet

The double crochet stitch (dc) is justifiably popular. Like the half double crochet, the yarn is wrapped around the hook before the hook is inserted into the stitch.

1. Wrap the yarn over the hook from back to front. Find the stitch where you will insert the hook. In the photo, it is the empty stitch next to the three (turning) chains. If you are working into already-made stitches like in this example, push the hook through both loops of the stitch. If you are working into the foundation chain, use only the top loop.

2. Push the hook through that stitch from front to back. Hold onto the finished work with your other hand to keep it from spinning and making it impossible to make the stitch. Use your hook hand to keep the loops on the hook from turning.

3. Wrap the yarn over (yo) the hook from back to front.

4. Pull the yarn through to the front. This leaves three loops remaining on the hook.

5. Wrap the yarn over the hook from back to front.

8. Pull through both loops.

6. Pull through two loops. This leaves two loops remaining on the hook.

9. This completes the double crochet stitch.

7. Wrap the yarn over the hook from back to front.

10. The top row on the swatch shows double crochet stitches.

To summarize: Wrap the yarn around the hook. Insert hook into stitch. Wrap yarn. Pull to front. Wrap and pull through two loops. Wrap and pull through two loops again.

Working in Rows

The important thing about working in rows is to keep them even. This can be tricky at the beginning and end of a row. Typically, you will make several chain stitches at the beginning of a row to equal the height of the stitches that will follow.

After you make your foundation chains, you will be instructed to work your first stitch a specified number of chains from the loop on the hook. This allows the last few chains—the number varies per stitch—to stand up straight and act as the first stitch in the row.

The same principle holds on subsequent rows. Chain stitches serve as placeholders for the first stitch. Here are guidelines for how many turning chains to make for the stitches used in this book. If you find that your stitches are too short or too tall, adjust the number of chains so your stitches are the same height as the others in the row.

Single crochet	1
Half double crochet	2
Double crochet	3

1. For practice, work a double crochet row. After the foundation chains, work your first stitch into the fourth chain from the hook. At the end of the row, chain stitch 3.

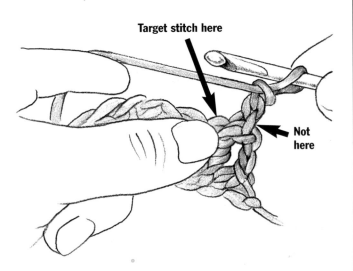

Target stitch here

Not here

Target stitch here

Not here

2. After you make the turning chains, do not insert the hook at their base. Because those chains count as a stitch, this would mean you would have two stitches where you should only have one, inadvertently increasing the number of stitches. If you notice that your work is getting wider, check to make sure you are not working a stitch at the base of the turning chain. Skip the base of the turning chains unless you are instructed otherwise.

3. At the far end of the row, work your last stitch into the topmost chain from the previous row; otherwise you will inadvertently decrease the number of stitches. If your work starts getting narrower, check to make sure you are working a stitch in this spot.

It does not matter whether you turn your work clockwise or counterclockwise, but it will look neater if you are consistent.

Joining a New Yarn

You will need to attach a new yarn when you run out of one skein or when you want to change colors. Here is the technique for attaching a new yarn without making any knots. It's best to join a new yarn at the beginning of a row if you can, but when that is not possible it is acceptable to join mid-row.

Different colors are used in the photos for instructional purposes; ordinarily you would not switch from one color to another in the middle of a row.

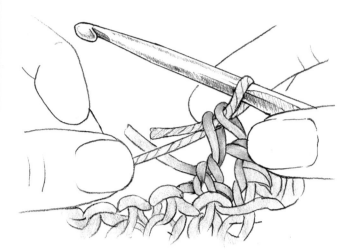

1. Work your stitch up to the next-to-last step. In other words, do not put the yarn over and pull through to complete the stitch. Let the old yarn hang to the back of the work.

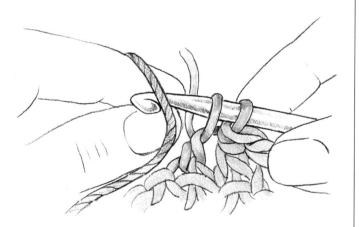

2. Put the new yarn over the hook and pull through to complete the stitch. Continue working with the new yarn, making sure you are using the working end of the yarn and not the short tail.

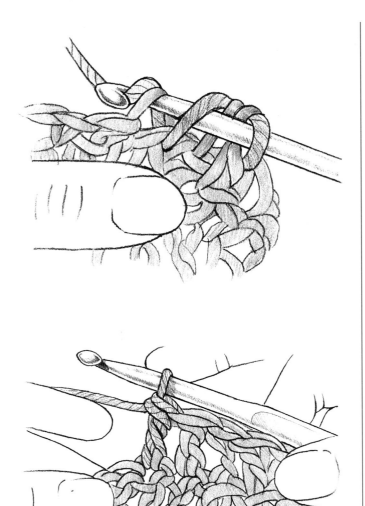

Notice that all parts of the first complete stitch with the new color are in that color, and no parts of the previous stitch are. Adding new yarn at the top of the previous stitch—as the last step in completing that stitch—has this happy result.

Fastening Off

This one is easy!

1. To end your work, cut the yarn about 2 inches from the hook.

2. Wrap the yarn around the hook and pull all the way through the loop so the tail comes through, too.

3. Pull to tighten.

Weaving in Ends

Finishing your work with care adds to its quality. It is not a good idea to knot your ends because they can come undone or can poke through to the right side of your work. Instead, weave the ends in by using a small crochet hook or a tapestry needle. Weave the ends through stitches on the wrong side of your work, then clip the ends close. Check to make sure no ends are visible on the right side.

TIP: You can hold short ends snugly next to the work and crochet subsequent stitches around them. This reduces the need to weave ends in when you finish the project.

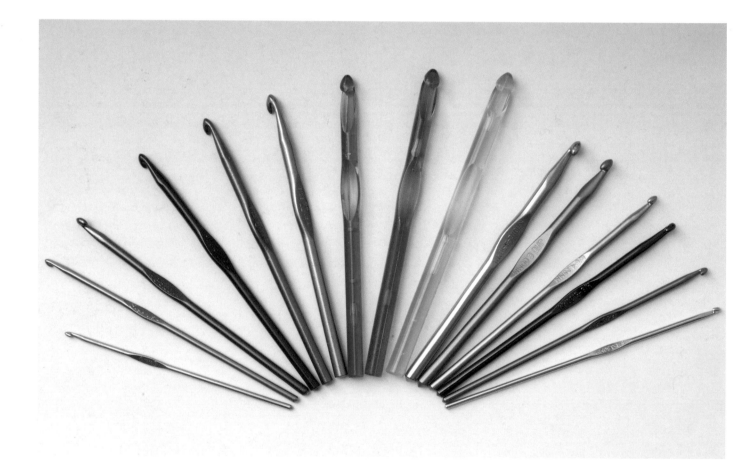

26

Measuring Gauge

Gauge is the number of stitches (or pattern repeats) and rows to a given measurement. Everyone crochets differently, so even if two people are using the same yarn, stitches, and hook, their gauges can vary.

For your work to be the right size, match the recommended gauge as closely as possible.

1. Work a swatch about 6 inches square, using the hook, yarn, and stitches that the pattern specifies.

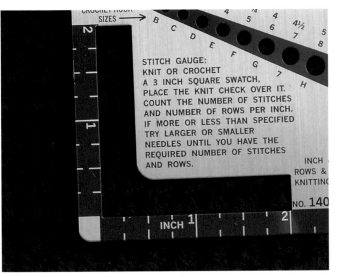

2. Using your gauge measurer, count the number of stitches and the number of rows you made, and compare this to the recommended gauge.

If you have more than you are supposed to, your gauge is too tight. Try again with a larger hook. If you have fewer rows or stitches than you are supposed to, your gauge is too loose. Try a smaller hook.

Sometimes your gauge is not equal horizontally and vertically. If you match better in one direction, it is more important to match the number of stitches than the number of rows.

When gauge is critical, like in a sweater, check gauge frequently when you start to work the pattern to verify that the gauge you calculated on the swatch is holding true for the garment. It is better to find out that your gauge is off early in a project than when it is too late to start over.

Blocking

Pieces often need to be blocked to smooth the stitches, shape a garment, make the corners square, flatten ends that are curling up, or obtain a professional finish. Here is an unblocked square. Notice how it curls up.

1. Lay each piece facedown on a padded surface like an ironing board cover. Using stainless steel pins, pin pieces in place, shaping them into the form they should be.

2. If you have a steam iron, hover it just above the cro-cheted pieces; the steam will set the stitches. Do not let the weight of the iron press the stitches, because it will flatten them. Another alternative is to place a damp cloth on top of the items. Gently place a warm iron down on the cloth, then lift it and move to another part of the item. Do not slide the iron around.

3. Let the pieces cool and dry before unpinning. The fabric will be nice and soft.

Block your gauge swatch to make sure it does not change your gauge. If it does, change your hook size accordingly.

Reading a Pattern

Crocheting uses standard abbreviations. Here is a list of the abbreviations used in this book (see also the master list in the appendix):

brdc	back raised double crochet (also called bpdc, back post double crochet)
ch	chain stitch
ch sp	chain space
dc	double crochet
dec	decrease
frdc	front raised double crochet (also called fpdc, front post double crochet)
hdc	half double crochet
rep	repeat
rnd	round
sc	single crochet
sk	skip
sl st	slip stitch
st	stitch
tog	together
yo	yarn over

Pattern books use parentheses ( ) or brackets [ ] to enclose a sequence of instructions meant to be repeated. After the closing parenthesis or bracket, you'll be told how many times to repeat the instructions.

For example, "[2 dc in next dc, 1 ch] twice" means to do 2 double crochet stitches in the next double cro-chet (from the row below), 1 chain stitch, 2 double cro-chet stitches in the next double crochet, 1 chain stitch.

Sometimes parentheses are just for explanatory in-formation. For example, "(the center of three double crochet stitches in the corner)" tells you the position of the stitch.

In this book, brackets are used for instructions to be repeated, and parentheses are used only for explanatory comments.

An asterisk * means to work the instructions follow-ing it as many more times as indicated. Sometimes the instructions will say, for example, "Repeat from * to end of row." You would keep doing the stitch or pattern fol-lowing the asterisk until you get to the end.

Part II

Projects

1

Shadowbox Pillow

Double crochet stitches worked with smooth yarn on a medium sized hook make this an ideal project for new crocheters. The result is a beautiful pillow that adds flair to any decor. Coffee-colored tones work well with the deep brown suede lacing.

Pillow Top (make 2)

Attach A to hook with slip knot. Chain 22.

Row 1: In fourth ch from hook, work 1 dc. Notice that the last three ch from the foundation row have turned upward to count as the first stitch in the row, and the dc you just made is the second stitch. Continue to work 1 dc into each ch across. The total will be 20 dc, including the one created by the turning chains.

Tip: Work into the top loop or both loops of the foundation chain, but be consistent with your chosen method. This option only applies for the first row. For the rest of the pillow, work through both loops of the existing stitches.

Row 2: Ch 3. Turn. The chains count as the first stitch, so do not work a dc in the base of the turning ch. (This would increase your count and give you too many stitches in the row. If you see your work starting to get wider, this is probably the mistake you're making.) Starting with the second stitch in the completed row below, work 1 dc in each stitch to end of row. The last stitch is worked into the top of the turning ch from the previous row. Total 20 dc made.

Rows 3–12: Repeat row 2. Count as you go along to make sure there are 20 stitches in each row. Fasten off by cutting yarn and pulling the tail through the loop.

Finished size: 16 inches square

Materials:

Caron Perfect Match, 7 oz./355 yards (198 g/325 meters), or similar 100 percent acrylic worsted weight yarn

1 skein of each:

Color A: Cream (7775)

Color B: Taupe (7751)

Color C: Espresso (7772)

Color D: Black (7718)

Hook: G or size needed to obtain gauge

Pillow form, 16 inches square

Suede lace: $^1/_8$ inch thick, dark brown (available at craft stores). The amount you need depends on how tightly you space the lacing. Five yards is more than enough.

Gauge: 6 double crochet stitches/2 inches, 2 double crochet rows/1 inch. Gauge is important so the pillow cover fits over the form.

Stitches and abbreviations:

Chain stitch (ch)

Double crochet (dc)

Tip: Examine your work periodically to make sure it is nice and square, with the ends of the rows lined up.

Row 13: With right side of square facing you (so the area you just fastened off is in the upper right for right-handers, upper left for left-handers), attach B to the last stitch from previous row with slip stitch. (Insert hook from front to back, loop yarn around, pull to front.) Ch 3. This counts as the first dc. Work 1 dc in each stitch across to end of row. Total 20 dc. Work 2 more dcs into same spot as last stitch, so there are 3 dc in the corner. This prevents the work from getting bunched up.

Now you will work down the side of the square. Look for the spaces at the end of each row. You will put your dcs into these spaces. Use the following pattern: 2, 2, 1. *Work 2 dc into first space, 2 dc into second space, 1 dc into third space. Repeat from * twice more. Work 2 dc into each of the last two spaces. This should bring you to the edge of the square.

Row 14: Ch 3, turn. Work 1 dc into next 19 dc for a total of 20 dc. In next stitch (corner), work 3 dc. Continue across second side working 1 dc into each stitch to end of row.

Row 15: Ch 3, turn. Work 1 dc into next 20 stitches for a total of 21 dc. In next stitch (corner), work 3 dc. Continue across second side, working 1 dc into each stitch to end of row.

Rows 16–20: Continue in same fashion, working 1 dc into each st along sides and 3 dc into each corner.

(Always work the 3 dc into the middle dc from the group of 3 in the previous row.) Fasten off.

Row 21: With right side of square facing you (so the fastened-off area is in upper right for right-handers, upper left for left-handers), attach C to last stitch from previous row with slip stitch. Ch 3. This counts as first dc. Work 1 dc in each stitch across the row, then 3 into the corner (the center stitch of the three in the corner of the previous row), then 1 dc into each stitch down the side.

Rows 22–28: Ch 3, turn. Work 1 dc into each st along sides and 3 dc into each corner. (Always work 3 dc into the middle dc from the group of 3 in the previous row.) Fasten off.

Row 29: With right side of square facing you (so the fastened-off area is in upper right for right-handers, upper left for left-handers), attach D to last stitch from previous row with slip stitch. Ch 3. This counts as first dc. Work 1 dc in each stitch across the row, then 3 into the corner (the center stitch of the three in the corner of the previous row, then 1 dc into each stitch down the side).

Rows 30–36: Ch 3, turn. Work 1 dc into each st along sides and 3 dc into each corner. (Always work the 3 dcs into the middle dc from the group of 3 in the previous row.) Fasten off.

Make second panel the same as the first.

Weave in ends. Block both pieces (see page 27) to get the corners sharp and the edges straight.

Finishing: Lay one of the squares right side down. Place pillow form on top. Lay the other square on top of pillow form, oriented so it matches the one underneath. You may leave the sides loose, gathering them together as you go along, or pin in place (leaving a small open area in one corner in which to hide the starting knot).

Cut a length of suede lace as long as you can comfortably work with (at least several feet). Make a knot at one end. Using a crochet hook, put knot between pillow and cover, then pull unknotted end of cord through the cover. From here on, use a whipstitch all around, joining top and bottom covers together. The whipstitch goes over both pieces that are to be joined in a spiral fashion. When the two parts of the pillow are lined up, pull the suede cord from the back to the front through both pieces, go over the top, and pull it through from back to front again. When you get all the way around, make another knot between pillow and cover. Cut excess suede. Tuck knot inside so it is not visible.

In this pillow, one color is fastened off before the next color is added.

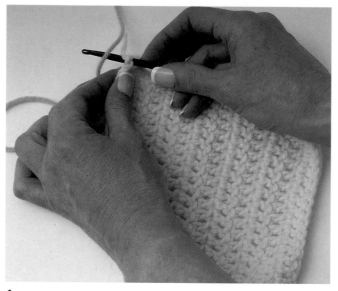

2. Put the yarn over again, making sure you are using the working end and not the tail. Pull through loop to complete the first chain stitch.

1. After fastening off one color, insert the hook from front to back in last stitch made (the same place you would put the hook if you had continued with the same color). Using the next color, put the yarn over the hook and pull through to the front. You do not need to make a knot.

3. Make 2 more chain stitches. These 3 chains count as the first double crochet in the row.

Use the same technique for the other colors. When you block the pillow top, it will be soft and flat.

4. Continue across the row. When you get to the corner, work 3 dc into the corner stitch. This keeps the work flat and the stitches even.

5. Work double crochet stitches evenly down the side of the square.

Shadowbox Pillow

1. Cut the suede cord to a length that is comfortable to work with. It should be at least several feet long to minimize the number of knots you need. Make a knot at one end.

2. With crocheted pillow cover pinned or held in place around pillow form, insert the cord so the knot is on the inside.

3. With crochet hook, pull cord through to front.

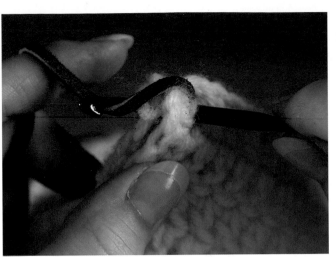

4. Put crochet hook through both pillow covers at the next lacing spot (approximately ½ to 1 inch down the side). Put cord over to the back, whipstitch fashion, and wrap around the hook. Pull through both pieces to front.

5. Continue lacing pillow all around. When you get back to the starting point, make another knot on the inside of the covers. Cut off extra suede. Tuck knots inside.

2
Jewel Tone Poncho

The jewel tone colors and rich texture in this yarn work up beautifully in double crochet stitches. The windowpane pattern creates a fashionable and comfortable poncho that's warm but not bulky.

Poncho Panel (make 2)

Tip: It takes practice to see where to put the hook when you use highly textured yarn. A large hook such as a size K makes it easier because the stitches and spaces are bigger. Use your fingers to feel for the spaces if they are obscured by the texture. Make sure you are going far enough before making the next stitch; otherwise you will inadvertently increase the number of stitches per row. After row 1, this gets much easier since you can use the stitches on the previous row as a guide. If you have trouble, practice the pattern with a smoother yarn first to get a feel for where the stitches are placed in the pattern, one windowpane row then two solid rows.

Attach yarn to hook with slip knot. Chain 37.

Tip: It is better to make a few extra chains than to be short. If you complete the next row and find you have extra chains, simply unknot them.

Row 1: Work 1 dc in fifth chain from hook. Ch 1. *Sk 1 chain, dc into next chain, ch 1. Repeat from * to last ch. Dc into last chain on foundation row. This should leave you with 17 windowpane spaces (18 dc total, including the dc formed by the initial turning ch).

Tip: Work into the top loop or both loops of the foundation chain, but be consistent with your chosen method. This option only applies for the first row. For the rest of the poncho, work through both loops of the existing stitches (or into windowpane space as instructed).

Row 2: Ch 3. Turn. These chains count as the first dc in the row. *Dc into first windowpane (yo, put hook from front to back through window, yo, pull to front, yo, pull through two loops, yo, pull through remaining two loops to make dc). Dc into top of dc below (both loops). Repeat from * all the way across. You will have 35 dc made, including the one from the initial turning chain.

Row 3: Ch 3. Turn. This counts as the first dc in the row. Do not work into the base of the turning chain. Dc

Finished size:

One size fits most adults. Each panel is approximately 16 x 34 inches. Back length: 25 inches from neckline to point, excluding fringe.

Materials:

Lion Brand Homespun, 6 oz./185 yards (170 g/169 meters)

Color 305 (Modern), 3 skeins

Hook: K or size needed to obtain gauge

Gauge: 4 dc stitches/1 inch, 1 dc row/1 inch. Gauge is flexible since one size fits all.

Stitches and abbreviations:

Chain stitch (ch)

Double crochet (dc)

Single crochet (sc)

Yarn over (yo)

Skip (sk)

into the top loops of each dc across. The final dc is worked into the top of the turning ch from the row below. Total 35 dc, including the stitch formed by the initial turning ch.

Row 4: Ch 4. Turn. This counts as the first dc in the row and the chain to make the top of the first windowpane. Do not work into the base of the turning chain.

Skip the next dc, then work 1 dc into the next dc. * Ch 1. Skip next dc, dc into next dc. Repeat from * across. Make sure that the windowpanes are right above the ones you made on row 1, the first windowpane row. Total 17 windowpanes (18 dc).

Repeat rows 2 to 4 until panel measures 34 inches long. Fasten off.

Make second panel the same as the first.

Finishing: Weave in ends. Line up the wrong sides of the short end of one panel with the long side of the second panel as shown.

Sew the first seam (approximately 16 inches) using the tapestry needle and matching yarn.

Turn poncho over (but do not invert inside to outside) and sew second seam, aligning the last row of the second panel with the side of the first. Make sure you do not sew either the neckline or the poncho sides; these must remain open.

Turn poncho right side out. Now you will crochet trim around the neck. Attach yarn at back bottom V of neckline. Work sc evenly spaced all the way around to neatly finish neckline. Fasten off. Weave in ends.

Attach fringe.

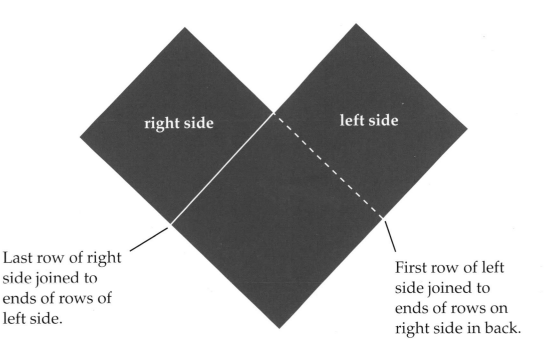

Last row of right side joined to ends of rows of left side.

First row of left side joined to ends of rows on right side in back.

A combination of double crochet and chain stitches creates attractive openwork.

Turn the work and make 4 chain stitches. The first 3 chains act as the vertical double crochet stitch at the beginning of the row. The fourth chain is the top of the windowpane. The tapestry needle indicates where you will place the next double crochet stitch. Do not work a dc into the base of the turning chain or the stitch after that.

Continue to work 1 ch, skip 1 dc below, dc into next dc. The windowpane pattern will start to emerge.

1. Each bunch of fringe has 3 strands doubled over to make 6 strands. Using a 6-inch long piece of cardboard, wrap yarn around three times, ending where you started.

2. Cut the bottoms to give 3 strands of equal length.

3. Fold the strands in half.

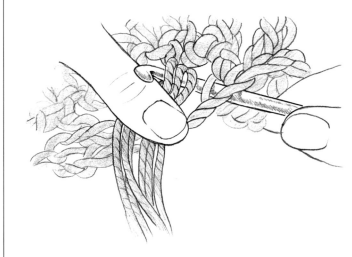

4. Using a crochet hook, pull the folded end through the windowpane at the front bottom point of the poncho from front to back.

Jewel Tone Poncho

43

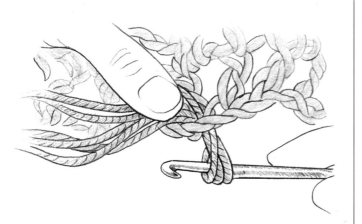

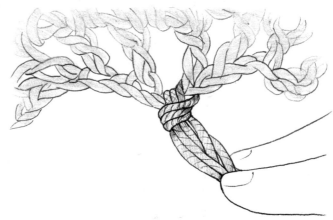

5. Hook the cut ends in a bunch. Pull them through the loop where the fringe is folded.

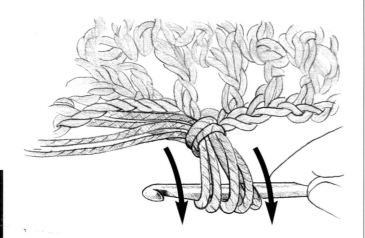

6. Continue to pull until ends come through. The fringe is now knotted in place.

7. Pull to tighten. Place fringe all along bottom edge of poncho, approximately every 2.5 inches. Trim ends to make fringe even.

3

Basketweave Blanket

Basketweave is created by working around the stems, or posts, of stitches to create a raised or relief effect. It's an ideal stitch for a yarn like this one that's not too simple, not too complicated. The shiny strand that's twisted with the solid color during the manufacturing process produces a subtle glow. Working the trim in a contrasting color gives this darling blanket a polished finish.

Blanket

Attach A to hook with slip knot. Chain 138.

Tip: If your base chains are usually tighter than the rest of your work, use one size larger hook for the chains. Switch back to the smaller hook for the next row.

Foundation row: Dc in fourth ch from hook. This counts as the second stitch; the last 3 chains will turn upward and count as the first stitch. Dc in each ch across. Total 136 dc, including the one formed by the initial chs.

Tip: It is better to make a few extra chains than to be short. If you complete the next row and find you have extra chains, simply unknot them.

Row 1: Ch 3. Turn. (Do not work a stitch into the base of the turning chain; those chains count as the first stitch, so if you put another stitch there you will inadvertently increase the number of stitches in the row.) Work 1 frdc around the post of each of the next 3 stitches from the row below. *Work 1 brdc around the post of each of the next 4 stitches from the row below, then 1 frdc around the post of each of the next 4 stitches from the row below. Repeat from * all the way across. The final brdc will be around the chains from the previous row (yo, insert hook from back to front, yo, pull through, yo, pull through two loops, yo, pull through remaining two loops to complete dc).

Tip: The stitches look different from the front and the back: they look like front raised stitches on one side and back raised stitches on the other.

Finished size: 38 inches square

Materials:

Bernat Baby Coordinates, 6 oz./185 yards (170 g/169 meters) sport weight yarn

Color A: Iced Mint (01012), 4 skeins

Color B: White (01000), 1 skein

Hook: G or size needed to obtain gauge

Gauge: One complete basketweave (4 back raised double crochet stitches and 4 front raised double crochet stitches)/2 inches; 8 rows in basketweave/3 inches. Gauge is somewhat flexible.

Stitches and abbreviations:

Chain stitch (ch)

Double crochet (dc)

Back raised double crochet (brdc); some patterns say back post double crochet (bpdc)

Front raised double crochet (frdc); some patterns say front post double crochet (fpdc)

Single crochet (sc)

Slip stitch (sl)

Yarn over (yo)

Row 2: Ch 3. Turn. Do not work a stitch into the base of the turning chain. Work 1 frdc around each of the next 3 frdc posts from the row below. *Work 1 brdc around each of the next 4 brdc posts from the row below, then 1 frdc around each of the next 4 frdc posts from the row below. Repeat from * all the way across. Work the last brdc around the chains from the previous row.

Rows 3 and 4: Repeat row 2.

Tip: Look at your work to make sure you have completed the first 4 rows of the basketweave properly: front raised stitches should be over front raised stitches; back raised stitches should be over back raised stitches. Now you will change the pattern to start the opposite part of the basketweave stitch.

Row 5: This is where the pattern switches to the opposite part of weave. Ch 3. Turn. Work 1 brdc around the posts of each of the next 3 frdc from the row below. *Work 1 frdc around the posts of each of the next 4 brdc from the row below. Work 1 brdc around the posts of each of the next 4 frdc from the row below. Repeat from * all the way across. Work the last frdc around the chains from the previous row.

Row 6: Ch 3. Turn. Work 1 brdc around the post of each of the next 3 brdc from the row below. *Work 1 frdc around the post of each of the next 4 frdc from the row below. Work 1 brdc around the posts of each of the next 4 brdc from the row below. Repeat from * all the way across, working the last stitch as described for previous rows.

Rows 7 and 8: Repeat row 6.

Rows: 9–104: Repeat rows 5–8. Fasten off.

This lightweight blanket is a thoughtful gift for a new baby.

TRIM

Row 1: Attach B to hook with slip knot. In the corner where you just ended A, work a slip stitch to attach B to blanket. Work 1 sc in the same space. Work 1 sc in each stitch all the way across top of blanket. Work 3 sc in corner. As you come down the side, space the sc stitches evenly so the trim lies flat with the blanket (approximately 112 stitches). Continue all the way around, working 3 sc in each corner. When you get back to the beginning, work 2 more sc into the corner where you did the original sc for a total of 3 sc in that corner. Join to the top of the first sc with a sl st.

Row 2: Ch 3. Turn. *Skip 1 sc. Work 1 sc into next sc. Skip 1 sc. Work 3 dc into next sc. Repeat from *, working 3 dc into each corner. When you get back to the beginning, work 2 more dc into the space with the initial ch 3. Join to top of chain with sl st. Fasten off.

Finishing: Weave in ends. Block blanket to make it nice and square (see page 27).

2. Continue with the double crochet stitch by putting the yarn over, then pulling through. Complete the stitch with the hook in this position. Work a total of 4 frdc for the first part of the basketweave, then switch to brdc to do the next part of the basketweave.

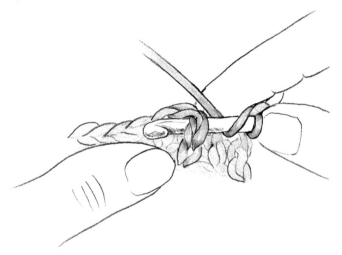

1. To work a front raised double crochet, yo, and then insert the hook from right to left around the post of the stitch below. The hook should start and end at the front of the work.

Tip: When you work front raised double crochet, tilt the work slightly away from you to make it easier for the hook to go behind the post and come out to the front again. When you work back raised double crochet, tilt the work slightly toward you to expose the back posts.

3. To work a back raised double crochet, yo, and then insert the hook from right to left around the post of the stitch below. The hook should start and end at the back of the work. In the photo and the illustration, the already-worked rows are bent to the back to show you where to place the hook.

Basketweave Blanket

After the specified number of rows, switch the pattern as instructed. This starts the next group of basketweave rows.

4. Continue with the stitch by putting the yarn over, then pulling through. Complete the stitch with the hook in this position. After you complete 4 brdc, switch back to frdc to continue the basketweave.

1. Attach yarn to hook with slip knot.

2. Attach yarn to corner of blanket with slip stitch.

4. Continue across. Work 3 sc in corner, then work evenly spaced sc stitches down the side.

3. Chain 1, then work a sc in the same space.

5. When you get back to the beginning, join yarn to initial chain with sl st.

Basketweave Blanket

6. Ch 3. Turn. The second row of trim has the following pattern: 1 sc stitch, then skip a stitch, then 3 dc worked in 1 stitch, then skip a stitch. Work 3 dc in each corner.

7. When you get back to the beginning, work 2 more dc into the space with the initial ch 3. Join to top of chain with sl st. Fasten off.

4

Horizontal Scarf

Let your creativity flow with novelty yarns for this fun and funky scarf. Use different colors and textures to get as fanciful as you please, or stick with one fluffy yarn for a more sophisticated look. The scarf is worked horizontally with built-in fringe. Simple single crochet stitches let the yarn speak for itself.

Scarf

Tip: It takes practice to see where to put the hook when you use highly textured yarn. A large hook such as a size K makes it easier because the stitches and spaces are bigger. Use your fingers to feel for the spaces if they are obscured by the texture. Make sure you are going far enough before making the next stitch; otherwise you will inadvertently increase the number of stitches per row. After row 2, this gets much easier since you can use the stitches on the previous row as a guide. If you have trouble, practice the pattern with a smoother yarn first to get a feel for where to place the stitches and how to start a new color.

Row 1: Attach A (Parrot) to hook with slip knot. Ch 16. Sl st into second ch from hook and each ch thereafter. This makes the first strand of fringe. Mark the last stitch here with a coilless safety pin or piece of contrasting yarn. Ch 116. Turn. Sl st into second ch from hook and next 14 stitches. (You'll be doubling back on the ch stitches you just made.) This makes the first strand of fringe at the opposite end. Mark this point with a safety pin or piece of contrasting yarn. There are 130 stitches total on each row: 15 fringe stitches on each end, 100 stitches of the scarf body between them. If you are using multiple colors, fasten off.

Tip: The fringe is built into this scarf, not added later. Each row starts with the fringe at one end, then the body, then the fringe at the other end.

Finished size:

Approximately 4 inches wide
x 60 inches long

Materials:

Plymouth Yarn

1 skein or ball of each:

Color A: Parrot, Item 941,
Color 2 (Bright Primary)

Color B: Outback Mohair,
Item 717, Color 895 (Rainbow)

Color C: Elegant, Item 943, Color 29
(Purple)

Color D: Eros Extreme, Item 942, Color
309 (Jewel Tones)

Color E: Meteor, Item 945,
Color 1518 (Magentas)

Note: If you prefer not to purchase full skeins of all the suggested yarns, this scarf is perfect for leftover or on-sale novelty yarn, or share yarn with a friend. For a subtler scarf, use just one kind of fluffy yarn. For example, Bernat Boa would be a practical and cost-effective substitution. You would need 2 skeins, each 71 yards (65 meters).

2 short pieces (3 inches each) of
contrasting color yarn, or 2 coilless safety
pins to use as markers

Hook: Size K

Gauge: Does not matter for this project

Stitches and abbreviations:

Chain stitch (ch)

Slip stitch (sl st)

Single crochet (sc)

Yarn over (yo)

Row 2: With right side facing, attach B (Outback Mohair) to hook with slip stitch. Insert hook through stitch at marker, where the fringe joins the scarf body. Yarn over, complete a slip stitch to attach to previous row. Ch 16 to start the fringe. Sl st into second ch from hook and each ch thereafter. This is the second strand of fringe. Move marker from first row to the spot where you just completed the fringe. Continue the row by working 1 sc into each of the 100 nonfringe stitches from first row. When you get to the end of that part, where the other marker is, ch 16. Sl st into second ch from hook and the next 14 ch to make 15 fringe stitches.

Rows 3–11: Repeat row 2, using the yarns in the following order

    Row 3, Eros Extreme (D)
    Row 4, Outback Mohair (B)
    Row 5, Elegant (C)
    Row 6, Meteor (E)
    Row 7, Outback Mohair (B)
    Row 8, Elegant (C)
    Row 9, Eros Extreme (D)
    Row 10, Outback Mohair (B)
    Row 11, Parrot (A)

Tip: You can change the order of the yarns if you like, but do rows 1 and 11 with the fluffiest yarn.

When you complete row 11, verify that there are 11 strands of fringe on each end. Fasten off. Weave in ends.

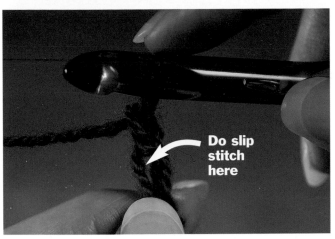

Do slip stitch here

1. Ch 16. The left thumbnail in the photo shows where you will begin doing the slip stitches to make the fringe. It is the second ch from the hook.

2. Work a slip stitch in that stitch and in all of the remaining stitches. This will give you 15 fringe stitches.

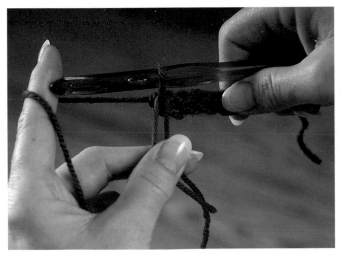

3. Place marker so you can tell where the fringe ends and the body of the scarf begins.

4. Ch 116. The first 100 stitches will be the body of the scarf; the last 16 will be worked with slip stitches to make 15 fringe stitches, just like the fringe at the first end. After completing the chain stitches, turn the work. Work a sl st in the second ch from the hook and each of the next 14 ch for a total of 15. Place another marker to indicate where the fringe ends and the body begins. If you are using more than one color, fasten off. With right side facing, attach next yarn at the marker (the rightmost marker for right-handers, leftmost marker for left-handers) and start with ch 16 to make fringe like on the first row. Work the slip stitches to complete that fringe. Next, work sc stitches in each of the 100 ch that make up the scarf's body, then ch 16 and sl st to make another fringe.

5

Bunny Basket

This festive basket introduces you to crocheting in the round, a skill that is also used for the hat, mittens, and the crocheted button on the handbag. Simple single crochet stitches let the colors take center stage. The blue and yellow shown here is just one successful combination; experiment with your own color duos to suit the season or your decor. The results will be as sweet as a chocolate bunny.

Basket

Attach two strands together (one of each color) to hook with slip knot. Ch 5. Sl st into the first chain you made. This forms a ring.

Round 1: Ch 1. Work 10 sc into center of ring. Sl st into initial ch to complete the round.

Round 2: Ch 1. Place marker. Do not work a stitch at the base of ch. Work 2 sc into each sc from previous round. Total 20 sc. Sl st into ch to complete round. Remove marker.

Tip: Remove the marker at the end of every round and replace it at the beginning of the next round.

Round 3: Ch 1. *Work 1 sc into first sc from previous round, then 2 sc into next sc from previous round. Repeat from * (1 sc, 2 sc, 1 sc, 2 sc, etc.) until the end of the round. Total 30 sc. Sl st into first ch to complete round.

Finished size:

Approximately 6 inches in diameter, 5 inches high (to top of handle)

Materials:

Royale Classic Crochet Thread, size 3 (100 percent mercerized cotton, 150 yards per ball)

1 ball of each:

Color A: Maize (0423)

Color B: Periwinkle (2221)

A short piece (2 inches) of contrasting color thread or one coilless safety pin to use as a marker

Hook: Size H

Tapestry needle

Gauge: Does not matter for this project

Stitches and abbreviations:

Chain stitch (ch)

Single crochet (sc)

Slip stitch (sl st)

Yarn over (yo)

Notes: To work two different colors together, you can make one two-colored ball before you begin, or simply work from two balls as you go along. No matter which method you choose, line up the ends when you attach the strands to the hook with the initial slip knot. Make sure you hook both strands as you go through the pattern.

When working in rounds, the right side is always facing you. Do not turn the work at the end of a round.

Starting with round 2, mark the beginning of each round by laying a short piece of contrasting color snugly against the round's initial chain stitch. Alternatively, you can use a coilless safety pin to mark this spot. At the end of each round, remove the marker and place it on the next round. This allows you to identify the beginning of the rounds easily, so you don't stop short or go too far.

Round 4: Ch 1. Work 1 sc into each sc from previous round. Total 30 sc. Sl st into first ch to complete round.

Round 5: Ch 1. *Work 1 sc into first sc from previous round, then 2 sc into next sc from previous round. Repeat from * (1 sc, 2 sc, 1 sc, 2 sc, etc.) until the end of the round. Total 45 sc. Sl st into first ch to complete round.

Round 6: Ch 1. Work 1 sc into each sc from previous round. Total 45 sc. Sl st into ch to complete round.

Round 7: Ch 1. *Work 1 sc into first sc from previous round, then 2 sc into next sc from previous round.

Repeat from * (1 sc, 2 sc, 1 sc, 2 sc, etc.) until the end of the round. Total 66 sc. Sl st into first ch to complete round.

Tip: When you stop increasing the number of stitches per round, the circle does not get any bigger. This allows the sides of the basket to form.

Rounds 8–16: Ch 1. Work 1 sc into each sc from previous round. Total 66 sc. Sl stitch into first ch to complete round. Do not fasten off.

Handle

The handle is not worked separately; it comes up right from one side of the basket.

Row 1: Ch 1. Do not stitch into base of ch. Work 1 sc into each of the next 5 sc. Turn.

Rows 2–36: Ch 1. Do not stitch into base of ch. Work 1 sc into each of the next 4 sc from previous row, then 1 sc into top of the ch from the previous row. Total 5 sc. Turn. Work enough rows so the handle measures approximately 10 inches. Fasten off, leaving a long tail (approximately 12 inches).

Finishing: Thread a tapestry needle with the long tail of both colors of yarn that are coming from the un-attached end of the handle. Make sure the basket is right side out. Position end of handle exactly opposite from where it starts. Sew the handle to the basket there. Weave in ends.

Tip: The "right side" is the side of the basket that was facing you when you worked the rounds. However, the important thing about the "right side" is that it is the side that looks best to you. Make sure that side of the basket faces outward.

To stiffen the basket, use starch according to the manufacturer's instructions. To get the right shape for the basket and handle, saturate it with starch and place it upside down over an appropriately shaped and sized bowl. Suspend the bowl over a bucket with a yardstick or ruler to keep it from falling in. Let dry.

Working two strands together in single crochet rounds creates a sturdy bowl for the basket.

Until now, you have been crocheting flat things. For three-dimensional objects such as baskets, hats, and mittens, you will work in circles (rounds) instead of rows.

1. Make the specified number of chain stitches.

2. Insert the hook into the first chain.

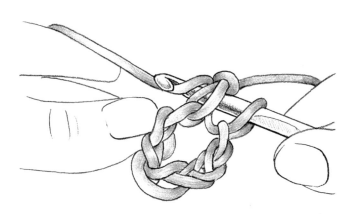

3. Wrap the yarn around the hook and pull through both loops to make a slip stitch. This creates a ring with a small hole in the middle.

4. Chain 1 to start the first round. Work the stitches by putting the hook through the hole from front to back, then wrapping the yarn over to begin your single crochet. Pull it to the front, then complete the stitch (yarn over and pull through both loops).

6. Join end of round to beginning by putting hook through the chain stitch you made at the beginning of the round and working a slip stitch.

5. Continue to work around the ring, pushing the stitches together if necessary, until you have done the specified number of stitches.

7. Work subsequent rounds in a similar fashion, but instead of putting the hook through the hole in the ring, insert it into the stitches from the previous round.

Bunny Basket

1. The handle emerges from the rim of the basket. There are no threads to cut or attach. After you have completed the round part of the basket, work single crochet stitches into the rim to make the beginning of the handle. Turn the work back and forth just like you would for any other crocheted rows.

2. When handle is desired length, cut a tail (both threads) approximately 12 inches long. Pull through loop on hook to fasten off. Thread a tapestry needle with both strands.

3. Position the end of the handle exactly opposite from where it starts. An easy way to do this is to fold the basket in half and match the handle ends. Pin in place if desired.

4. With the outside of the basket facing you, whipstitch the handle to the basket rim. A whipstitch is done by putting the needle through both stitches, pulling taut, then going through both stitches again in the same direction.

5. When handle is sewn on, make a slip knot in the thread without unthreading it from the needle. Slide the needle through several stitches on the inside of the basket where the handle meets the rim. Trim thread closely to complete the project.

6

Child's Watch Cap

This cozy hat can be made on its own or to go with the mittens in chapter 7. Working in just one loop of each stitch creates the ribbed effect on the cuff.

Finished size: See below

Instructions are given for four ages/sizes:

Ages 3/4 [head circumference 14.25 in./36.5 cm; hatband depth (unfolded) 3.75 in./9.6 cm; crown depth 4.25 in./10.9 cm]

Ages 5/7 [head circumference 16 in./41 cm; hatband depth (unfolded) 4.25 in./10.9 cm; crown depth 4.5 in./11.5 cm]

Ages 8/10 [head circumference 17.75 in./45.5 cm; hatband depth (unfolded) 4.75 in./12.2 cm; crown depth 5.25 in./13.5 cm]

Ages 12/14 [head circumference 19.5 in./50 cm; hatband depth (unfolded) 5.25 in./13.5 cm; crown depth 5.5 in./14.1 cm]

Note: Head sizes vary greatly among children; a 3-year-old can have a larger head than a 7-year-old. To get the best fit, measure the child's head and pick the most appropriate size.

Materials (enough for hat and mittens on page 72):

Kraemer Yarns Summit Hill 100 percent Merino Superwash Wool, 3.5 oz./230 yards

KTX1110 Aquamarine or KTX1108 Garnet: 1 skein for sizes 3/4 and 5/7; 2 skeins for 8/10 and 12/14.

Hook: G or size needed to obtain gauge

Short piece (2 inches) of contrasting color yarn or a coilless safety pin to use as a marker

Tapestry needle

Gauge: For the cuff, 9 back loop sc or 9 hdc/1 inch; 4 patterns (1 row back loop only sc, 1 row hdc)/2 inches

Stitches and abbreviations:

Chain stitch (ch)

Single crochet (sc)

Back loop only (blo)

Half double crochet (hdc)

Yarn over (yo)

Tip: In the instructions, the first number of stitches or rows is for size 3/4. The number for the larger sizes is given in parentheses. For example:

Work a total of 16 (18, 20, 22) rows

means work 16 rows for size 3/4, 18 rows for size 5/7, 20 rows for size 8/10, and 22 rows for size 12/14. Before you start making the hat, go through the pattern and circle in pencil the numbers for your desired size. This will help you avoid mixing sizes accidentally by reading the wrong number.

Hatband

Tip: The hatband is worked sideways. The first row will be joined to the last row to make it into a circle.

Attach yarn to hook with slip stitch. Chain 18 (20, 22, 24).

Row 1: Work 1 hdc into third ch from hook. (The last 3 chains count as the first hdc stitch.) Work 1 hdc into each ch to end. Total 16 (18, 20, 22) stitches.

Row 2 (wrong side): Ch 1. Turn. Work 1 sc into back loop only of next hdc and into each hdc to end of row.

Tip: Count your stitches on each row to make sure you are not increasing or decreasing. If you find you are increasing, you are probably working a stitch at the base of the turning chain where it does not belong. If you are decreasing, you are probably neglecting to work a stitch at the end of a row into the top of the turning chain below. Keeping your stitch count consistent will make your work look nice and neat.

Row 3 (right side): Ch 2. Turn. Work 1 hdc into the next sc and into each sc to end of row.

Work rows 2 and 3 a total of 32 (36, 40, 44) times for a total of 64 (72, 80, 88) rows.

The ribbing on the hatband is achieved by working in the back loop of the stitches.

JOINING END OF HATBAND TO BEGINNING

With right sides together, insert hook into back loop of next hdc, then into the corresponding loop (the one closest to the one you just hooked) in the ch st from first row. Yarn over, pull through, yo, pull through both loops. Repeat to end of row. Do not fasten off.

Tip: Make sure the hatband is the right size. If possible, have the child try it on. Make any necessary adjustments to the cuff (adding rows or pulling them out) before you proceed.

Crown

Turn cuff so wrong side is facing out. (The wrong side is the less visibly ribbed side. You want it facing out now because when you're done, you'll fold up the cuff and the nicely ribbed side will show.)

Ch 1. Work 64 (72, 80, 88) sc evenly around entire edge of cuff.

Tip: Mentally divide the edge of cuff into quarters. Work 16 (18, 20, 22) sc into each quarter and you'll get the correct total.

The hatband can be folded up . . . or not!

Do not join with a slip stitch when you get back to the beginning. Just keep working 1 sc in each stitch, spiral fashion. Place marker at beginning of each new round, moving when you get to the next round, so you can easily count the number of rounds you have worked. Work 12 (13, 15, 16) rounds.

Next round: You will start decreasing the number of stitches per round by skipping a sc from the previous round as instructed. *Work 1 sc into each of the next 9 (10, 11, 12) stitches. Skip 1 sc. Repeat from * until round is 28 (32, 35, 39) stitches around, or until crown of hat reaches desired depth to top of head.

Hat Tip

Next round: *Work 1 sc into each of the next 5 (6, 6, 7) stitches. Skip 1 --sc. Repeat from * until 8 (9, 9, 11) stitches remain at the tip of the hat. Fasten off, leaving an 8-inch tail. Thread the tail into the darning needle. Draw through all of the remaining stitches, pull to inside of hat to close. Weave in end on the inside of hat. Trim excess.

The ribbed-cuff hat is soft, stretchy, and warm.

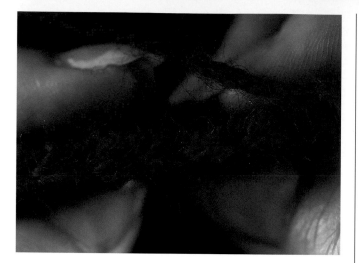

1. Insert the hook from front to back through the back loop only (blo) of the half double crochet stitch from the previous row.

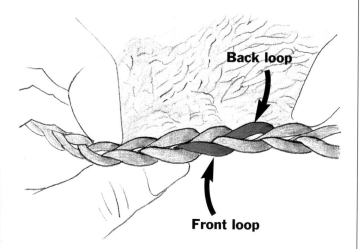

Each stitch consists of two loops. Look down from the top. The front loop is the one closer to your thumbs. The back loop is the one closer to your fingers. Usually you put the hook under both loops, but by working through just one loop you can create a ribbed effect. You will work sc stitches into the back loop only (blo) to create the ribbed hatband in this project.

2. Yarn over, pull through. Yarn over, pull through both loops to complete the single crochet. Alternating back loop only rows with regular (both loops) rows creates this ribbed effect.

1. With right sides together, line up final row of hatband with the first row.

2. *Insert hook through back loop of hdc and front loop of chain stitch. Yarn over, pull through. Yarn over, pull through both loops to complete the stitch. Repeat from * to end of row. Fasten off.

7

Child's Mittens

The perfect complement to the watch cap are these matching mittens, which require making a thumb gusset and crocheting the thumb.

Finished size: See below

Instructions are given for four ages/sizes:

Ages 3/4 (cuff diameter 3.5 in./9 cm; cuff length 3.75 in./9.6 cm; hand length 4 in./10.3 cm)

Ages 5/7 (cuff diameter 4 in./10.3 cm; cuff length 4.25 in./10.9 cm; hand length 4.5 in./11.5 cm)

Ages 8/10 (cuff diameter 4.5 in./11.5 cm; cuff length 4.75 in./12.2 cm; hand length 5 in./12.8 cm)

Ages 12/14 (cuff diameter 5 in./12.8 cm; cuff length 5.25 in./13.5 cm; hand length 5.5 in./14.1 cm)

Materials (enough for the mittens and the hat on page 65):

Kraemer Yarns Summit Hill 100 percent Merino Superwash Wool, 3.5 oz./230 yards

KTX1108 Garnet or KTX1110 Aquamarine: 1 skein for sizes 3/4 and 5/7; 2 skeins for 8/10 and 12/14

Hook: G or size needed to obtain gauge

Short piece (2 inches) of contrasting color yarn or a coilless safety pin to use as a marker

Tapestry needle

Gauge: For the cuff, 9 back loop sc or 9 hdc/1 inch; 4 patterns (1 row back loop only sc, 1 row hdc)/2 inches

Stitches and abbreviations:

Chain stitch (ch)

Single crochet (sc)

Back loop only (blo)

Half double crochet (hdc)

Yarn over (yo)

Skip (sk)

Tip: In the instructions, the first number of stitches or rows is for size 3/4. The number for the larger sizes is given in parentheses. For example:

Work 18 (20, 22, 24) stitches

means work 18 stitches for size 3/4, 20 stitches for size 5/7, 22 stitches for size 8/10, and 24 stitches for size 12/14. Before you start making the mittens, go through the pattern and circle in pencil the numbers for your desired size. This will help you avoid mixing sizes accidentally by reading the wrong number.

Cuff (make 2)

Tip: The cuff is worked sideways. The first row will be joined to the last row to make it into a circle.

Attach yarn to hook with slip stitch. Chain 18 (20, 22, 24).

Row 1: Work 1 hdc into third ch from hook. (The last 3 chains count as the first hdc stitch.) Work 1 hdc into each ch to end. Total 16 (18, 20, 22) stitches.

Row 2 (wrong side): Ch 1. Turn. Work 1 sc into back loop only of next hdc and into each hdc to end of row.

Tip: Count your stitches on each row to make sure you are not increasing or decreasing. If you find you are increasing, you are probably working a stitch at the base of the turning chain where it does not belong. If you are decreasing, you are probably neglecting to work a stitch at the end of a row into the top of the turning chain below. Keeping your stitch count consistent will make your work look nice and neat.

Row 3 (right side): Ch 2. Turn. Work 1 hdc into the next sc and into each sc to end of row.

Work rows 2 and 3 a total of 8 (9, 10, 11) times for a total of 16 (18, 20, 24) rows.

Getting ready to face the elements.

JOINING END OF CUFF TO BEGINNING

With right sides together, insert hook into back loop of next hdc, then into the corresponding loop (the one closest to the one you just hooked) in the ch st from first row. Yarn over, pull through, yo, pull through both loops. Repeat to end of row. Do not fasten off.

Tip: Measure to make sure the cuff is the right size. If possible, have the child try it on. Make any necessary adjustments to the cuff (adding rows or pulling them out) before you proceed. Cuffs are worn unfolded—nice and long so the mittens stay on little hands.

Palm

Make sure right side of cuff is facing out. (The right side is the more visibly ribbed side. Because the cuff is not folded, you want that side facing out so it will show when the mitten is done.)

Ch 1. Work 28 (32, 35, 39) sc evenly around entire edge of cuff.

Do not join with a slip stitch when you get back to the beginning. Just keep working 1 sc in each stitch, spiral fashion. Place marker at beginning of each new round by laying yarn between the last and first stitches. Move the marker when you get to the next round, so you can easily count the number of rounds you have worked. Work 4 (5, 5, 6) rounds.

Next round: Now you will leave a space for the thumb. Ch 4 (5, 5, 6) sc, sk 4 (5, 5, 6) stitches, 1 sc in each stitch around to where the chain stitches start. Work 4 (5, 5, 6) sc into the ch space, then 1 sc in each sc for an additional 12 (13, 15, 16) rounds or until mitten reaches tip of pinkie finger.

Next round: You will start decreasing the number of stitches per round by skipping a sc from the previous round as instructed. *Work 1 sc into each of the next 5 (6, 6, 7) stitches. Skip 1 sc. Repeat from * until 8 (9, 9, 11) stitches remain at tip of mitten. Fasten off, leaving an 8-inch tail. Thread the tail into the darning needle. Draw through all of the remaining stitches and pull to inside of mitten to close. Weave in end on the inside of mitten. Trim excess.

Thumb

Join yarn at right edge of thumb opening. Sc 12 (14, 14, 16) stitches around thumb opening.

Next round: Skip 1 sc, work 1 sc into each of the next 5 (6, 6, 7) stitches. Do this twice. Next, skip 1 sc, work 1 sc into each of the next 4 (5, 5, 6) stitches. Do this twice. Work 1 sc into each of the remaining stitches for 6 (7, 7, 8) rounds or until thumb is desired length.

Next round: 1 sc, skip 1 to end of round. Fasten off, leaving an 8-inch tail. Thread the tail into the darning needle. Draw through all of the remaining stitches, pull to inside of mitten to close. Weave in end on inside of mitten. Trim excess.

1. When you get to where the thumb should be placed, chain the number of stitches specified in the pattern. Skip the single crochet stitches below.

2. Continue with sc stitches after you have skipped the right number below.

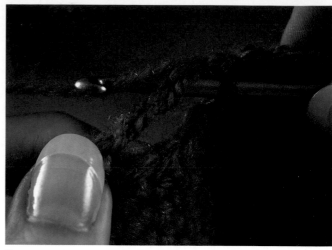

3. When you get around to where the chains are, work the specified number of sc into the space made by the chains.

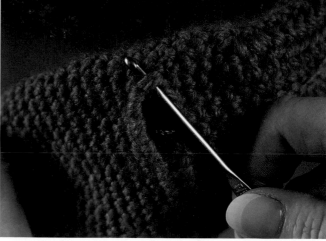

4. After you finish the mitten palm, you will need to start a new piece of yarn to make the thumb. Put the hook through the right side of the thumb opening. Pull a loop of yarn through. Yarn over, pull through loop to attach the yarn.

5. Continue to work the specified number of sc stitches, skipping stitches to decrease as indicated in pattern.

6. When you have decreased to the number of sc stitches indicated in the pattern, fasten off. Thread the tail through a tapestry needle. Work needle through all remaining stitches. Put needle to inside of mitten. Pull to close the hole.

8

Openwork Placemats

This delicate style of openwork and closed blocks is called "filet," from the French for "net." Chain stitches and double crochets create a meshwork pattern. Filet designs can be floral, pictorial, or geometric. These placemats use a simple pattern of airy and solid squares that looks at home on any table.

Placemat (make 4)

Join A to hook with slip knot. Ch 87.

Tip: If your chains are usually tighter than the rest of your work, use one size larger hook for the chains. Switch back to the smaller hook for the next row.

Tip: It is better to make a few extra chains than to be short. If you complete the next row and find you have extra chains, simply unknot them.

Row 1: Dc in fourth chain from hook. The first 3 ch count as the first dc in the row, so when you make your dc you will now have 2 complete dc. Dc in each of the next 5 chain stitches, for a total of 7 dc. *[Ch 1. Sk 1 ch from the row below. Dc in next chain] three times. You will have three "holes." Dc into each of the next 6 chains. Repeat from * all the way across, ending with an openwork section.

Tip: Your pattern will have a solid bank of stitches, then an openwork one, then solid. When you count the solid stitches, there will be 7 in each group—one as the end to the openwork section and 6 for the solid section. There will be three holes in each openwork section.

Finished size: 12 x 16 inches

Materials:

Royale Fashion Crochet Thread 100 percent mercerized cotton, article 164, size 3, 150 yards/137 meters)

Color A: 6 balls for a set of 4 placemats

Color B: 1 ball to trim 4 placemats

Samples are worked in Bridal White, Scarlett, and Navy

Hook: F or size needed to obtain gauge

Gauge: 5 dc/inch; 2.5 rows/inch

Stitches and abbreviations:

Chain stitch (ch)

Double crochet (dc)

Single crochet (sc)

Yarn over (yo)

Skip (sk)

Filet placemats dress up a summer table.

Row 2: Ch 4. Turn. This counts for the first dc and 1 ch. Skip the base of the turning ch and 1 more ch, then dc into the next dc from the row below. Ch 1, skip the ch below, dc into the dc below twice, for a total of three open blocks. *Work 1 dc into the each of the next 6 dc below. Ch 1, skip ch below, dc into ch below three times. Repeat from * until end of row. The final dc is worked into the top of the turning ch from the row below, so you will end with a solid block of 7 dc.

Note: You will see the pattern emerging: openwork over openwork, solid over solid. Stop to make sure that you have the right number of open groups and the right number of solid blocks.

Row 3: Ch 3. Turn. This counts for the first dc. Do not work a stitch into base of turning ch. *Dc into each of the next 6 dc below. [Ch 1, skip 1 ch from the row below, dc into dc below] three times. Repeat from * across, ending with openwork pattern (ch 1, sk ch from row below, 1 dc in dc below).

When you are done row 3, you have finished the first set of stitches. Rows 4, 5, and 6 will be the opposite of those rows: you will have solid blocks of dc in rows 4 to 6 where you had openwork in rows 1 to 3, and openwork on rows 4 to 6 where you had solid blocks in rows 1 to 3.

Don't worry about stains—this cotton is machine washable.

Row 4: Ch 3. Turn. This counts as the first dc. Do not work a stitch into the base of the turning ch. (Work 1 dc into open space below by putting the hook right into the space, not through the ch stitch, then 1 dc into top of dc from row below) three times. This will give you a solid block of 7 dc, including the turning ch.

*[Ch 1, skip 1 dc below, dc into the next dc below] three times. [Dc into the open space below, dc into next dc] three times. Repeat from * across, ending with openwork pattern (ch 1, sk dc below, dc into next dc) three times. The last dc will be into the top of the turning ch from the row below.

Stop and look at your work. Make sure you have changed the pattern starting with row 4.

Row 5: Repeat row 2.

Row 6: Repeat row 3.

Rows 7–30: Repeat rows 4 through 6. Check your work frequently to make sure you have been consistent with the pattern. Fasten off.

TRIM

Arrange placemat so openwork squares are in upper right (or upper left for left-handers). You will work across a long side first.

With a slip stitch, attach contrasting color to hook as follows: Put hook through corner block from front to back, yo, pull to front, yo, pull through loop. Ch 1. Work 2 sc in same open block. Total 3 sc. [Work 2 sc into next open block] twice.

*[Work 1 sc into the space between the next 2 dc] six times. Work 2 sc into each of the next three open blocks. Repeat from * to end of row. Work 2 more sc into space between last 2 dc.

Turn to work down the short side of the placemat. Work 1 more sc into same space where the 3 sc made the turn. Total 4 sc in that space. *Work 2 sc into each of next three open blocks. [Work 2 sc into the space left between the dc stitches] three times. Repeat from * to end of row. In the corner, work 2 more sc for a total of 4.

Continue down the next long side. Work 2 sc into each of the next two open blocks. *[Work 1 sc into the space between the next 2 dc] six times. Work 2 sc into each of the next three open blocks. Repeat from * to end of row. Work 2 more sc into space between last 2 dc.

Turn to work down the remaining short side. Work 1 more sc into same space where the 3 sc made the turn. Total 4 sc in that space. *Work 2 sc into each of next three open blocks. [Work 2 sc into the space left between the dc stitches] three times. Repeat from * to end of row. When you get to the last block, sc 1, then join with sl st to the first sc you made with the trim color. Fasten off. Weave in ends.

Finishing: Block placemat so the edges are square and the sides are straight. (See page 27.)

SKILL WORKSHOP: FILET CROCHET

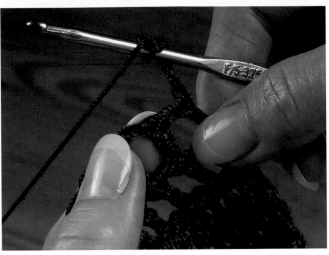

1. This shows how to work openwork over openwork. Ch 4. The first three chains act as the vertical bar of a dc; the fourth ch is the horizontal bar that makes the top of the openwork.

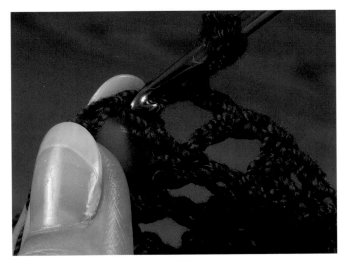

2. Work a dc into the top of the dc from the openwork row below.

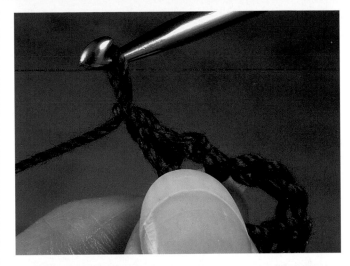

3. Ch 1. Work a dc into the top of the next dc below.

4. When you complete the openwork section, work 1 dc into the top of each dc below to work solid section.

83

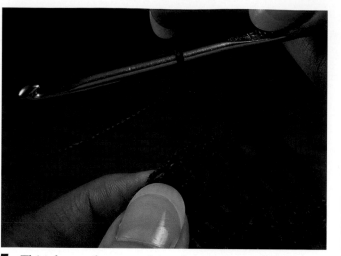

5. This shows the row where the pattern switches to openwork over solid. Ch 4. Skip the base of the turning ch and the next dc below, then work 1 dc into next dc from below.

6. To work solid over openwork, work 1 dc in the open hole, the next dc in the top of the dc below, next dc in the open hole, etc.

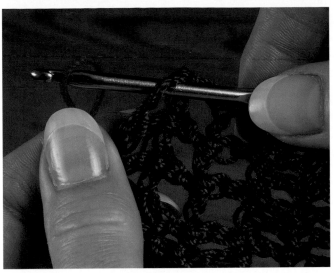

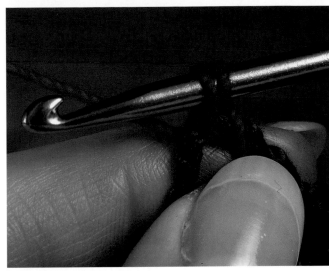

1. Attach yarn to hook with slip stitch as follows. Put hook through corner block from front to back, yo, pull to front, yo, pull through loop. Ch 1.

2. Work 2 more sc in that space. Work sc across top and down side as specified in pattern. When you get back to the beginning, join to initial ch with a sl st.

9

Woven Shoulder Bag

Handbags have to be sturdy and stylish. Woven stitch, a combination of single crochets and chain stitches, accomplishes both goals beautifully. Single crochets are worked into the spaces on the row below, giving strength to the weave. Woven stitch is interesting enough to use with a smooth, solid color yarn and also shows off more highly textured yarn such as chenille to great advantage. A crocheted button closure completes this practical and fashionable shoulder bag.

Shoulder Bag

Tip: Bag is worked as one piece (front, back, flap) and then the side seams are sewn.

Attach yarn to hook with slip knot. Chain 40.

Tip: If your chains are usually tighter than the rest of your work, use one size larger hook for the chains. Switch back to the smaller hook for the next row.

Tip: It is better to make a few extra chains than to be short. If you complete the next row and find you have extra chains, simply unknot them.

Row 1: Work 1 sc in second ch from hook, *ch 1, skip 1 ch, work 1 sc in next ch. Repeat from * to end of row. You will have made 20 sc.

Row 2: Ch 1. Turn. Skip first sc (the one that was at the end of the first row, which is now the base of the turning ch), *1 sc in 1 ch sp immediately after the sc you skipped, ch 1, skip 1 sc, repeat from *, ending 1 sc in 1 ch (the turning ch from the row below). Total 20 sc made.

Finished size:

6.5 inches high x 9 inches wide. Bag hangs 11.5 inches from top of strap.

Materials:

Caron Perfect Match, 7 oz./355 yards (198 g/325 meters), or similar 100 percent acrylic worsted weight yarn

Taupe (7751), 1 skein

Hook: G or size needed to obtain gauge

Tapestry needle

Gauge: Make a swatch of woven stitch to measure your gauge. 4 complete woven stitches (each is 1 single crochet and 1 chain stitch)/2 inches; 8 woven stitch rows/2 inches

Stitches and abbreviations:

Chain stitch (ch)

Chain space (ch sp)

Decreasing single crochet (dec sc)

Single crochet (sc)

Slip stitch (sl st)

Yarn over (yo)

These fashion-savvy handbags go with everything.

Rows 3–46: Repeat row 2.

Now you are going to start decreasing stitches from each end, to make the front flap come to a point. You will do this by working 2 sc into 1 at each end.

Row 47: Ch 1, turn. Work one decreasing sc into the first two stitches. Ch 1. Skip the sc below. *1 sc in ch space, 1 ch, skip 1 sc. Repeat from * until there is 1 ch sp and the turning ch remaining on the previous row. Work 1 dec sc into that ch sp and turning ch.

Row 48–54: Repeat row 47.

Tip: After each row, check to make sure you are decreasing at the same rate on each side so the triangular flap will look neat. Do this by folding the work lengthwise; edges should match.

Row 55: Work 1 decreasing sc into last two stitches. Ch 11 to make loop for closure. Join with a sl st to the same spot where the ch started. Fasten off.

Strap

Attach yarn to hook with slip knot. Ch 135 (or the number of ch you need to make a length 32 inches long). If your chain row is usually tighter than the rest of your work, use one size larger hook for the chains, then switch back to the smaller hook. This will prevent your strap from being lopsided.

Row 1: Sc in second ch from hook and every chain to the end.

Row 2: Ch 1. Turn. Sl st into every stitch to end of row. Fasten off.

Crocheted Button

Attach yarn to hook with slip knot, leaving about an 8-inch tail. Chain 4. Join ends with sl st, making tiny circle.

Round 1: Make sure you are using the working yarn, not the tail. Ch 1. Work 12 sc into the circle. (Put hook through circle, yo, pull back through circle, 2 loops on hook. Yo, pull through both loops to complete sc.) Push the stitches back toward the beginning so you have enough space to make all 12. Join with sl st to top of first sc. Do not turn.

Round 2: Ch 1. *Work 1 sc in next st, then 2 sc in next st. Repeat from * to end of round. Total 18 sc. Join to top of first sc with sl st. Do not turn.

Round 3: Ch 1. This starts to tighten the button. Skip first st, then work 1 sc in next stitch. Continue to work 1 sc every other stitch all the way around. Total 9 sc. Fasten off, leaving about an 8-inch tail.

Thread the tail onto a tapestry needle. Use a crochet hook to pull the initial tail of thread through. Now, using the tapestry needle, work the thread through the 9 stitches around the circle, then pull tight. You will have two lengths of thread sticking out from the center of the button.

A crocheted button makes a nice closure, or use a large button or bead instead.

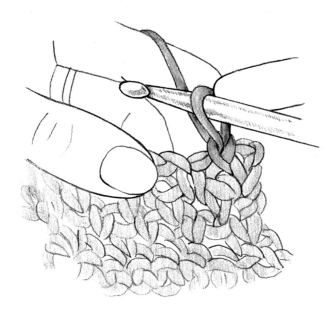

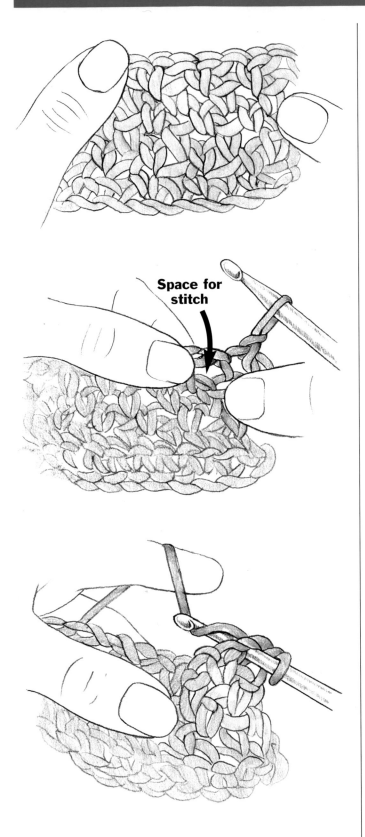

Space for stitch

1. Woven stitch places single crochet stitches into the chain spaces from the row below. After initial chains are made, work 1 sc in second ch from hook. *Ch 1, skip 1 ch, 1 sc in next ch. Repeat from * to end.

2. Ch 1. Turn. Skip first sc. *1 sc in ch sp, ch 1, skip 1 sc. Repeat from *, ending with 1 sc in ch.

Woven Shoulder Bag

2. Insert hook into next ch sp. Yo and pull through. Three loops on hook.

1. Insert hook into first ch sp. Yarn over and pull through. Two loops on hook.

3. Yarn over and pull through all three loops.

4. This completes the decreasing single crochet.

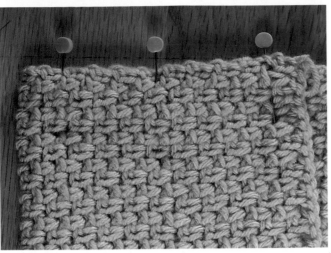

1. Block bag and strap (see page 27). Lay body of bag wrong side down. Fold bottom up to meet the place where the flap (decrease) starts. Pin seams.

3. Place or pin 2 inches on each end of handle to side seam of bag. Make sure that handle is not twisted. Sew handle onto seam, starting the thread at the top of the bag, working down 2 inches to the bottom of the handle, then sewing across the bottom of the handle and up the other side.

2. Thread a tapestry needle with the same type of yarn you used for the bag. Knot thread. Starting at the bottom, sew side seams, putting the needle through one loop of a sc on front and one loop of a sc on back of bag.

4. Turn bag right side out. Close the flap. With a pin or crochet hook, mark where the loop hits the bag so you know where to sew the button on.

5. Open the flap. Using the two tails from the button, pull through to inside (one tail on each side of a stitch, not through the same spot). Turn the bag inside out enough so you can make a knot inside with those two ends after you pull them through firmly.

6. Weave in any loose ends. Close the loop over the button.

10
Wavy Sweater

W avy chevron stitches—really just double crochets arranged in an interesting pattern—give this sweater a little stretch. The finished product is fitted without being clingy, comfortable without being boxy. A scalloped waistline and double crochet trim around the neckline add to the professional, stylish look. Follow the instructions and your sweater will look gorgeously handcrafted, not "homemade."

Finished size: S, M, or L

Instructions are given for sizes small, medium, and large. See the sizing chart in the Appendices to choose the correct finished size for you.

Materials:

Plymouth Encore, 3.5 oz./200 yards, or similar 75 percent acrylic, 25 percent wool knitting worsted weight yarn

4 skeins of each:

Color A: Blue (2946)

Color B: Gold (175)

Color C: Red (174)

Note: You may need an extra skein for the sleeve color.

Hook: I or size needed to obtain gauge

Tapestry needle

Gauge: Gauge is very important for this project! If you ignore it, you risk ending up with a sweater that's either huge or doll size. Crochet a swatch of wavy chevron stitches and a swatch of regular double crochet stitches, then check your gauge so you can adjust your hook size if necessary. Check again after completing a few rows of the back of the sweater, and again when you make the sleeves. If your gauge is off, it's better to find out early so you can make adjustments, rather than when it's too late to start over.

Gauge for sleeve: 10 dc stitches/3 inches; 6 dc rows/3 inches

Gauge for back and front of sweater: 1 complete chevron (from top of one chevron to the top of the next, total 10 dc stitches)/3 inches; 5 chevron rows/3 inches

Stitches and abbreviations:

Chain stitch (ch)

Double crochet (dc)

Slip stitch (sl st)

Two double crochet together (2 dc tog)

Tip: In the instructions, the first number of stitches or rows is for size S. The number for the larger sizes is given in parentheses. For example:

Work a total of 1 (2, 3) rows

means work 1 row for size small, 2 for medium, 3 for large. Before you start making the sweater, go through the pattern and circle in pencil the numbers for your desired size. This will help you avoid mixing sizes accidentally by reading the wrong number.

Wavy Sweater

Back

Attach A to hook with slip knot. Ch 48 (56, 64).

Row 1: Ch 3 more to count as turning ch. Dc at the base of the turning ch (fourth ch from hook) so it looks like 2 stitches are made in the same space, in a V shape. *Dc in next ch. [Dc over 2 stitches (this is the same as double crochet 2 stitches together)] twice. Dc in next ch. [Work 2 dc in next ch] twice. Repeat from *, ending with the first pair of 2 dc worked in 1 stitch. Fasten off.

Row 2: Join B. Ch 3. 1 dc at base of turning ch. *1 dc in next dc. [2 dc tog] twice. Dc in next dc. [Work 2 dc in next dc] twice. Repeat from *, ending with the first pair of 2 dc worked in 1 stitch. Fasten off.

Tip: Make sure you are working 2 dc tog into 1 TWICE, as indicated. If your chevron gets out of kilter, forgetting to do this is the likely culprit.

Row 3: Repeat with C.

Rows 4–19 (approximately): Repeat row 3, using color sequence A, B, C, until back measures 13 (13.5, 14) inches, or desired length to underarm. Fasten off.

BACK ARMHOLE SHAPING

Note: If you look at the back of a sweater, you will see that it narrows when it gets to the underarm. That's what you will do at this point.

Next row: With the right side of the sweater back facing you, find the trough in the first chevron stitch from the right. (Left-handers may prefer to go the opposite direction but should still have the outer, or "right," side of the garment facing them.) There are two pairs of 2 dc tog at the base of this trough. Locate the leftmost pair. Continuing with the appropriate color in the stripe sequence, attach the yarn here. Ch 3. This counts as the first dc. Continue in chevron pattern. Stop after working 2 dc tog into the right-hand pair of 2 dc tog in the final trough. There will be the same number of unworked stitches at each end of the row.

Next row: Continue in pattern until back measures 17.5 (18, 18.5) inches from beginning. Fasten off.

BACK SHOULDER SHAPING

Note: Here you are going to work the ends of the garment, but not the middle. This gives some shaping to the back of the neckline, making it dip a little from the shoulders. The front neckline is worked differently so it will be slightly lower than the back, as in most sweaters.

Row 1: Continuing in stripe sequence, and with right side of garment facing you, join yarn to rightmost edge as usual for a new row. Work 10 (15, 20) stitches in the chevron pattern. (Remember, 2 dc worked tog counts as 1 stitch.) Work 1 (2, 3) rows. Fasten off.

With right side facing, count back from the other edge 10 (15, 20) stitches. Join same color yarn that you used on the first shoulder, and continue in chevron pattern to end of row. The number of stitches you make should be the same for the left shoulder and the right shoulder. Work the same number of rows as for other shoulder. Fasten off.

The armhole shaping begins in the trough of the first chevron.

Front

Work as Back until Armhole Shaping.

FRONT ARMHOLE SHAPING

Next row: Find the trough in the first chevron stitch from the right. (Left-handers may prefer to go the opposite direction.) There are two pairs of 2 dc tog at the base of this trough. Locate the leftmost 2 dc tog. Continuing with the appropriate color in the stripe sequence, attach the yarn there. Ch 3. This counts as the first dc. Continue in chevron pattern. Stop after working 2 dc tog into the right side of the final trough. There will be unworked stitches at each end of the row.

Next row: Continue in pattern until front measures 16 (16.5, 17) inches from beginning. Fasten off.

FRONT SHOULDER SHAPING

Note: Here you are going to work the ends of the garment, but not the middle. This gives some shaping to the center of the neckline. The front neckline will be slightly lower than the back, as in most sweaters.

Row 1: Continuing in stripe sequence, and with right side of garment facing you, join yarn to rightmost edge as usual for a new row. Work 10 (15, 20) stitches in the chevron pattern. (Remember, 2 dc worked tog counts as 1 stitch.)

Row 2: Ch 3. Turn. Continue in stripe sequence, working chevron pattern in all of the stitches from row 1. The shoulder will be getting longer here. Work the number of rows needed so total rows from bottom of front to top of shoulder lines up with corresponding number of rows on back. Fasten off.

Next row (other shoulder): With right side facing, count back from the other edge 10 (15, 20) stitches. Join same color yarn that you used on the first shoulder, and continue in chevron pattern all the way to the end of the row. There are unworked stitches in the middle of the row (front of neck). The number of stitches should be the same for the left shoulder and the right shoulder. Work the same number of rows as for other shoulder. Fasten off.

Tip: Lay your pieces together and make sure there are the same number of rows from the bottom of each piece to the start of the armholes, and from the start of the armholes to the top of the shoulder. You want everything to match up when you assemble the pieces. The front neckline will be slightly lower than the back.

Sleeve (make 2)

Note: If you want to get wild (or use your yarn up more evenly), crochet each sleeve in a different color.

Attach A to hook with slip knot. Chain 27 (29, 31).

Row 1: Dc in fourth chain from hook and in all of the other chains. Total 24 (26, 28) dc made.

Row 2: Ch 3. Turn. The ch 3 counts as the first stitch. Dc in next dc and in each dc across, including into the top of the turning ch from the previous row.

Row 3: Repeat row 2.

Row 4: Ch 3. Turn. Here you will increase the number of stitches in the row to start making the sleeve wider. To do this, work the first dc into the base of where you just made the turning chain. Dc across to end (only 1 dc in turning ch at end of row). Total 25 (27, 29) dc made.

Row 5: Repeat row 4. Total 26 (28, 30) dc made.

Rows 6–7: Repeat row 3 (no increase).

Rows 8–9: Repeat row 4 (increase 1).
Continue 2 rows without increasing, then 2 rows increasing 1 dc at the beginning of the row. Do this until sleeve measures 17 (17.5, 18) inches to underarm.

Tip: Measure the sleeve against your arm periodically to make sure it fits the way you like. If it is getting too wide, increase only every third or fourth row. If it is too tight, increase more frequently. Balance the increases so they are not always at the same end of the work.

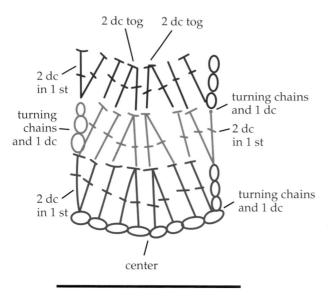

1. Start by chaining a multiple of 8 stitches, plus 3 more ch to count as the first dc.

Wavy chevron diagram

Wavy Chevron

Tip: The waves in this stitch are made by working 2 dc into one stitch at the crests of the chevrons, and joining 2 dc into 1 stitch at the bases. You will always start the pattern either at a crest or a trough, never in the middle.

Keep a rhythm to the stitches. I say, "Two, one, two; two, one, two" in my head when I work the pattern. It means:

Two	2 double crochet stitches in 1 stitch at the crest to make a V-shape
One	1 double crochet in the next stitch
Two	2 doubles worked together (turns 2 stitches into one to make an upside-down V) in the trough
Two	2 more doubles worked together (turns 2 stitches into 1) in the trough
One	1 double crochet in the next stitch
Two	2 double crochet stitches made in the next stitch

2. Dc in the fourth chain from hook. This acts like having 2 dc come out of the same stitch to form the V at the top of the crest.

3. 1 dc in next ch.

4. [Work 2 dc tog over next 2 ch] twice. To work double crochets together, work the first dc up to where the last yo, pull through remaining loops will complete it, but don't do that part. Instead, work the next dc in the next stitch. For the final step, pull through all of the loops on the hook. You have just worked 2 dc tog. This technique is used to decrease the number of stitches in a row.

5. 1 dc in next ch.

6. 2 dc in next ch.

For subsequent rows, ch 3. Work 1 dc in first dc (makes V of 2 stitches), 1 dc in next dc, [2 dc tog over next 2 st] twice, 1 dc in next dc, 2 dc in next dc, *2 dc in next dc, 1 dc in next dc, [2 dc tog over next 2 sts] twice, 1 dc in next dc, 2 dc in next dc. Repeat from *, working the last 2 dc in the top of the turning ch.

Wavy Sweater

1. Block all of the sweater pieces to size. (See p. 27.)

2. With right sides together, line up the front and back of the sweater. Trim the ends to 1 to 2 inches.

3. Using a tapestry needle, sew the shoulder tops and side seams together. Position the ends of the yarn you just trimmed so the yarn from the seaming holds them in place. Remember not to sew the armholes closed.

4. Fold each sleeve so the right sides are inside. Using a tapestry needle and matching yarn, sew the seams on the sleeves.

Wavy Sweater

5. Pin the sleeves into place. Using a tapestry needle, sew the sleeves to the armholes. Make sure you do not sew the armholes closed in the process.

6. Weave in any loose ends. Turn sweater right side out. Add trim around the neckline in whichever color you like best, as follows: Attach yarn at top of one shoulder seam. Ch 3. Work 1 row of dc all the way around. If your stitches seem to gap in the neckline corners, work 2 dc tog to decrease the number of stitches there. If your stitches seem to pull anywhere, work 2 dc into one stitch to relieve this.

When you get all the way around, join to the top of the ch 3 with a sl st. Fasten off. Weave in ends.

Appendices

Crocheting Abbreviations Master List

Following is a list of crochet abbreviations used in patterns by yarn industry designers and publishers. The most commonly used abbreviations are highlighted. In addition, designers and publishers may use special abbreviations in a pattern, which you might not find on this list. Generally, a definition of special abbreviations is given at the beginning of a book or pattern.

Abbreviation	Description
[ ]	work instructions within brackets as many times as directed
( )	work instructions within parentheses as many times as directed
*	repeat the instructions following the single asterisk as directed
* *	repeat instructions between asterisks as many times as directed or repeat from a given set of instructions
"	inch(es)
alt	alternate
approx	approximately
beg	begin/beginning
bet	between
BL	back loop(s)
bo	bobble
BP	back post
BPdc	back post double crochet
BPsc	back post single crochet
BPtr	back post treble crochet
CA	color A
CB	color B
CC	contrasting color
ch	chain stitch
ch-	refers to chain or space previously made: e.g., ch-1 space
ch-sp	chain space
CL	cluster
cm	centimeter(s)
cont	continue
dc	double crochet
dc2tog	double crochet 2 stitches together
dec	decrease/decreases/decreasing
dtr	double treble
FL	front loop(s)
foll	follow/follows/following
FP	front post

Abbreviation	Description
FPdc	front post double crochet
FPsc	front post single crochet
FPtr	front post treble crochet
g	gram
hdc	half double crochet
inc	increase/increases/increasing
lp(s)	loops
m	meter(s)
MC	main color
mm	millimeter(s)
oz	ounce(s)
p	picot
pat(s) or patt	pattern(s)
pc	popcorn
pm	place marker
prev	previous
rem	remain/remaining
rep	repeat(s)
rnd(s)	round(s)
RS	right side
sc	single crochet
sc2tog	single crochet 2 stitches together
sk	skip
Sl st	slip stitch
sp(s)	space(s)
st(s)	stitch(es)
tch or t-ch	turning chain
tbl	through back loop
tog	together
tr	treble crochet
trtr	triple treble crochet
WS	wrong side
yd(s)	yard(s)
yo	yarn over
yoh	yarn over hook

Skill Levels for Crocheting

SKILL LEVELS FOR CROCHET

1	■□□□	Beginner	Projects for first-time crocheters using basic stitches. Minimal shaping.
2	■■□□	Easy	Projects using yarn with basic stitches, repetitive stitch patterns, simple color changes, and simple shaping and finishing.
3	■■■□	Intermediate	Projects using a variety of techniques, such as basic lace patterns or color patterns, mid-level shaping and finishing.
4	■■■■	Experienced	Projects with intricate stitch patterns, techniques and dimension, such as non-repeating patterns, multi-color techniques, fine threads, small hooks, detailed shaping and refined finishing.

Most crochet and knitting pattern instructions will provide general sizing information, such as the chest or bust measurements of a completed garment. Many patterns also include detailed schematics or line drawings. These drawings show specific garment measurements (bust/chest, neckline, back, waist, sleeve length, etc.) in all the different pattern sizes. To insure proper fit, always review all of the sizing information provided in a pattern before you begin.

Following are several sizing charts. These charts show Chest, Center Back Neck-to-Cuff, Back Waist Length, Cross Back, and Sleeve Length **actual body measurements** for babies, children, women, and men. These measurements are given in both inches and centimeters.

When sizing sweaters, the fit is based on actual chest/bust measurements, plus ease (additional inches or centimeters). The first chart entitled "Fit" recommends the amount of ease to add to body measurements if you prefer a close-fitting garment, an oversized garment, or something in-between.

The next charts provide average lengths for children's, women's and men's garments.

Both the Fit and Length charts are simply guidelines. For individual body differences, changes can be made in body and sleeve lengths when appropriate. However, consideration must be given to the project pattern. Certain sizing changes may alter the appearance of a garment.

HOW TO MEASURE

1. Chest/Bust
Measure around the fullest part of the chest/bust. Do not draw the tape too tightly.

2. Center Back Neck–to-Cuff
With arm slightly bent, measure from back base of neck across shoulder around bend of elbow to wrist.

3. Back Waist Length
Measure from the most prominent bone at base of neck to the natural waistline.

4. Cross Back
Measure from shoulder to shoulder.

5. Sleeve Length
With arm slightly bent, measure from armpit to cuff.

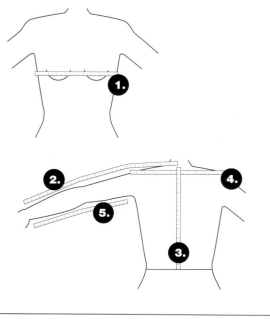

FIT

Very-close fitting: Actual chest/bust measurement or less
Close-fitting: 1–2"/2.5–5cm
Standard-fitting: 2–4"/5–10cm
Loose-fitting: 4–6"/10–15cm
Oversized: 6"/15cm or more

LENGTH FOR CHILDREN

Waist length: Actual body measurement
Hip length: 2"/5cm down from waist
Tunic length: 6"/15cm down from waist

LENGTH FOR WOMEN

Waist length: Actual body measurement
Hip length: 6"/15cm down from waist
Tunic length: 11"/28cm down from waist

LENGTH FOR MEN

Men's length usually varies only 1–2"/ 2.5–5cm from the actual "back hip length" measurement (*see chart*)

Baby's size	3 months	6 months	12 months	18 months	24 months
1. Chest (in.)	16	17	18	19	20
(cm.)	*40.5*	*43*	*45.5*	*48*	*50.5*
2. Center Back Neck-to-Cuff	10½	11½	12½	14	18
	26.5	*29*	*31.5*	*35.5*	*45.5*
3. Back Waist Length	6	7	7½	8	8½
	15.5	*17.5*	*19*	*20.5*	*21.5*
4. Cross Back (Shoulder to shoulder)	7¼	7¾	8¼	8½	8¾
	18.5	*19.5*	*21*	*21.5*	*22*
5. Sleeve Length to Underarm	6	6½	7½	8	8½
	15.5	*16.5*	*19*	*20.5*	*21.5*

Child's size	2	4	6	8	10
1. Chest (in.)	21	23	25	26½	28
(cm.)	*53*	*58.5*	*63.5*	*67*	*71*
2. Center Back Neck-to-Cuff	18	19½	20½	22	24
	45.5	*49.5*	*52*	*56*	*61*
3. Back Waist Length	8½	9½	10½	12½	14
	21.5	*24*	*26.5*	*31.5*	*35.5*
4. Cross Back (Shoulder to shoulder)	9¼	9¾	10¼	10¾	11¼
	23.5	*25*	*26*	*27*	*28.5*
5. Sleeve Length to Underarm	8½	10½	11½	12½	13½
	21.5	*26.5*	*29*	*31.5*	*34.5*

Standard Body Measurements/Sizing continued

Child's (cont.)	12	14	16
1. Chest (in.)	30	31½	32½
(cm.)	*76*	*80*	*82.5*
2. Center Back Neck-to-Cuff	26	27	28
	66	*68.5*	*71*
3. Back Waist Length	15	15½	16
	38	*39.5*	*40.5*
4. Cross Back (Shoulder to Shoulder)	12	12¼	13
	30.5	*31*	*33*
5. Sleeve Length to Underarm	15	16	16½
	38	*40.5*	*42*

Woman's size	X-Small	Small	Medium	Large
1. Bust (in.)	28–30	32–34	36–38	40–42
(cm.)	*71–76*	*81–86*	*91.5–96.5*	*101.5–106.5*
2. Center Back Neck-to-Cuff	27–27½	28–28½	29–29½	30–30½
	68.5–70	*71–72.5*	*73.5–75*	*76–77.5*
3. Back Waist Length	16½	17	17¼	17½
	42	*43*	*43.5*	*44.5*
4. Cross Back (Shoulder to Shoulder)	14–14½	14½–15	16–16½	17–17½
	35.5–37	*37–38*	*40.5–42*	*43–44.5*
5. Sleeve Length to Underarm	16½	17	17	17½
	42	*43*	*43*	*44.5*

Woman's (cont.)	1X	2X	3X	4X	5X
1. Bust (in.)	44–46	48–50	52–54	56–58	60–62
(cm.)	*111.5–117*	*122–127*	*132–137*	*142–147*	*152–158*
2. Center Back Neck-to-Cuff	31–31½	31½–32	32½–33	32½–33	33–33½
	78.5–80	*80–81.5*	*82.5–84*	*82.5–84*	*84–85*
3. Back Waist Length	17¾	18	18	18½	18½
	45	*45.5*	*45.5*	*47*	*47*
4. Cross Back (Shoulder to Shoulder)	17½	18	18	18½	18½
	44.5	*45.5*	*45.5*	*47*	*47*
5. Sleeve Length to Underarm	17½	18	18	18½	18½
	44.5	*45.5*	*45.5*	*47*	*47*

Man's Size	Small	Medium	Large	X-Large	XX-Large
1. Chest (in.)	34–36	38–40	42–44	46–48	50–52
(cm.)	*86–91.5*	*96.5–101.5*	*106.5–111.5*	*116.5–122*	*127–132*
2. Center Back Neck-to-Cuff	32–32½	33–33½	34–34½	35–35½	36–36½
	81–82.5	*83.5–85*	*86.5–87.5*	*89–90*	*91.5–92.5*
3. Back Hip Length	25–25½	26½–26¾	27–27¼	27½–27¾	28–28½
	63.5–64.5	*67.5–68*	*68.5–69*	*69.5–70.5*	*71–72.5*
4. Cross Back (Shoulder to Shoulder)	15½–16	16½–17	17½–18	18–18½	18½–19
	39.5–40.5	*42–43*	*44.5–45.5*	*45.5–47*	*47–48*
5. Sleeve Length to Underarm	18	18½	19½	20	20½
	45.5	*47*	*49.5*	*50.5*	*52*

Head Circumference Chart

	Infant/Child				Adult	
	Premie	**Baby**	**Toddler**	**Child**	**Woman**	**Man**
6. Circumference						
(in.)	12	14	16	18	20	22
(cm.)	*30.5*	*35.5*	*40.5*	*45.5*	*50.5*	*56*

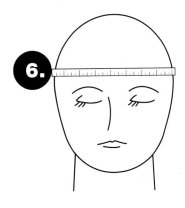

For an accurate head measure, place a tape measure across the forehead and measure around the full circumference of the head. Keep the tape snug for accurate results.

Standard Yarn Weight System

Categories of yarn, gauge ranges, and recommended needle and hook sizes

Yarn Weight Symbol & Category Names	① Super Fine	② Fine	③ Light	④ Medium	⑤ Bulky	⑥ Super Bulky
Type of Yarns in Category	Sock, Fingering, Baby	Sport, Baby	DK, Light Worsted	Worsted, Afghan, Aran	Chunky, Craft, Rug	Bulky, Roving
Knit Gauge Range* in Stockinette Stitch to 4 inches	27–32 sts	23–26 sts	21–24 sts	16–20 sts	12–15 sts	6–11 sts
Recommended Needle in Metric Size Range	2.25–3.25 mm	3.25–3.75 mm	3.75–4.5 mm	4.5–5.5 mm	5.5–8 mm	8 mm and larger
Recommended Needle U.S. Size Range	1 to 3	3 to 5	5 to 7	7 to 9	9 to 11	11 and larger
Crochet Gauge* Ranges in Single Crochet to 4 inch	21–32 sts	16–20 sts	12–17 sts	11–14 sts	8–11 sts	5–9 sts
Recommended Hook in Metric Size Range	2.25–3.5 mm	3.5–4.5 mm	4.5–5.5 mm	5.5–6.5 mm	6.5–9 mm	9 mm and larger
Recommended Hook U.S. Size Range	B–1 to E–4	E–4 to 7	7 to I–9	I–9 to K–10½	K–10½ to M–13	M–13 and larger

* GUIDELINES ONLY: The above reflect the most commonly used gauges and needle or hook sizes for specific yarn categories.

Resources

BOOKS

Barnden, Betty. *The Crochet Stitch Bible*. Iola, WI: Krause Publications, 2004.

Curtis, Carol. *Carol Curtis' Complete Book of Knitting and Crocheting*. New York: Pocket Books, 1954.

Davis, Jane. Crochet: *20 Simple and Stylish Designs to Wear*. New York: Lark Books, 2001.

Eckman, Edie. *The Crochet Answer Book*. North Adams, MA: Storey Publishing, 2005.

Huxley, Susan. *Crocheted Sweaters: Simple Stitches, Great Designs*. Woodinville, WA: Martingale & Company, 2001.

———. *Today's Crochet: Sweaters from the Crochet Guild of America*. Woodinville, WA: Martingale & Company, 2003.

Knight, Erika. *Simple Crochet*. New York: Clarkson Potter, 2003.

Leisure Arts. *Creative Crochet*. Little Rock, AR: Leisure Arts, 1996.

Matthews, Anne. *Vogue Dictionary of Crochet Stitches*. Newton, UK: David & Charles, 1987.

Reader's Digest. *The Ultimate Sourcebook of Knitting and Crochet Stitches*. Pleasantville, NY: Reader's Digest, 2003.

Swartz, Judith L. *Hip to Crochet: 23 Contemporary Projects for Today's Crocheter*. Loveland, CO: Interweave Press, 2004.

Whiting, Sue. *Learn to Crochet*. Upper Saddle River, NJ: Creative Arts & Crafts, 2003.

YARN AND CROCHETING SUPPLIES

Your local yarn shop is the best source for supplies and advice. The staff is knowledgeable about yarns from many different manufacturers and can help you substitute one yarn for another or find just the right color combination. Questions are welcomed and advice is given freely. Check the shop's schedule for specialty classes to add to your skill set, and get on the mailing list so you find out when yarn is on sale.

Catalogs and online retailers sell yarn and equipment. Hundreds of providers exist; you can find them on the Internet by searching for "yarn," "crocheting," or "free patterns." Here are just a few sources.

Art Yarns
914-428-0333
www.artyarns.com

Bernat
888-368-8401
www.bernat.com

Berroco Yarns
508-278-2527
www.berroco.com

Caron
www.caron.com

Classic Elite Yarns
978-453-2837
www.classiceliteyarns.com

Coats & Clark (includes Royale Crochet Thread)
800-648-1479
www.coatsandclark.com

Herrschners
800-441-0838
www.herrschners.com

Himalaya Yarn
802-862-6985
www.himalayayarn.com

Interlacements
719-578-8009
www.interlacementsyarns.com

Kraemer Yarns
800-759-5601
www.kraemeryarnshop.com

Lion Brand Yarn Company
800-258-9276
www.lionbrand.com

Mary Maxim Exclusive Needlework and Crafts
800-962-9504
www.marymaxim.com

Patternworks
800-438-5464
www.patternworks.com

Plymouth Yarn Company
215-788-0459
www.plymouthyarn.com

Yarn Market
888-996-9276
www.yarnmarket.com

OTHER RESOURCES FOR CROCHETERS

Craft Yarn Council of America
The craft yarn industry's trade association has educational links and free projects.
www.craftyarncouncil.com

Crochet Guild of America
The national association for crocheters and the publisher of *Crochet!* magazine. The association sponsors conventions, offers correspondence courses, and maintains a membership directory.

Interweave Press
Although more focused on knitting and other fiber arts than crocheting, Interweave publishes a special issue of their *Interweave Knits* magazine dedicated to crocheting.
www.interweave.com

Stackpole Basics

All the Skills and Tools You Need to Get Started

- **Straightforward, expert instruction on a variety of crafts, hobbies, and sports**
- **Step-by-step, easy-to-follow format**
- **Current information on equipment and prices for the beginner**
- **Full-color photography and illustrations**
- **Convenient lay-flat spiral binding**